A MOTHERS HEART

Holding onto Hope, Believing for a Baby

By

CHEREE MORTON

A Mother's Heart: Holding onto Hope, Believing for a Baby

Copyright 2026 by Cheree Morton

Cover design: Zolten Hercik
Interior layout and formatting: Dawn Black

Many thanks to my dear Sisters in Christ who edited this book: Wendy Nix and Marianne Peterson and too my beautiful Sister Kiah Woodall for being the first to give her heart to Jesus through these pages.

Forward

A Mothers Heart is a powerful invitation to renew your mind and align your heart with what God has already promised. Cheree's testimony carries hope, clarity, and spiritual authority, helping readers recognise that God is more committed to their breakthrough than they may realise. As you read, faith rises and lies lose their power, reminding you that God's promises and your prayers are actively working right now. The message in this book will awaken confidence, expectancy, and joyful trust in God's perfect timing.

Steve Backlund
Igniting Hope Ministries

It was such an honour to read Cheree's book, A Mother's Heart. This book is not merely written, it is released by God for such a time as this. In an hour where the lives of the unborn are under such threat and the value of children is increasingly diminished, the message carried within these pages stands as a call to awaken and contend for life through prayer, hope and faith. What God has breathed through this book will not only bring healing and revelation to mothers, but will also be used to release and preserve a multitude of newborn lives for generations to come.

I have been blessed to walk with Cheree for many years and I have witnessed her unwavering faith, obedience and intimacy with God as she has journeyed through this calling. Her words carry truth, testimony, hope and redemption.

As you read A Mother's Heart, be prepared for God to move miraculously in and through you. This book invites you into alignment with God's perspective over your womb, your legacy and your faith.

Mighty Woman of God, there is a miracle waiting to be birthed both physically and spiritually and this book will stir your heart to believe, contend and partner with God for all He has promised.

Marianne Petersen
Principal of Her Harvest Global Academy &
Founder of Kairos Creative Studio

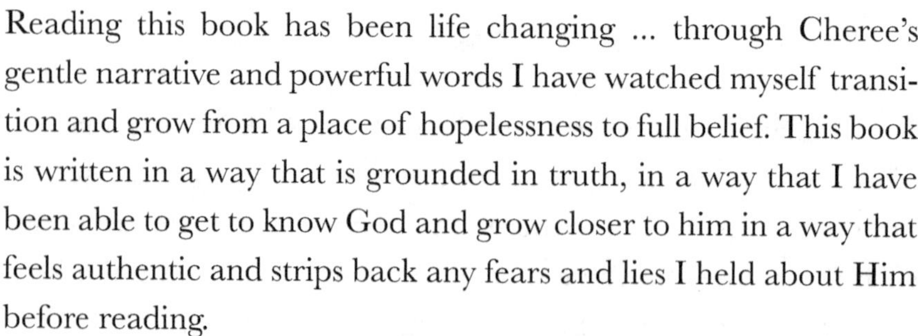

Reading this book has been life changing ... through Cheree's gentle narrative and powerful words I have watched myself transition and grow from a place of hopelessness to full belief. This book is written in a way that is grounded in truth, in a way that I have been able to get to know God and grow closer to him in a way that feels authentic and strips back any fears and lies I held about Him before reading.

Through doing the activations I have uncovered something deep within me, I have peeled back layers of lies that were embedded in past trauma and I have grown into a new way of thinking, new perspective and have began developing a gentle love for myself through connection to spirit and God.

I have endometriosis and am mid-thirties as I write this, I have never been able to fall pregnant and this has painted the narrative in my mind that I never will, what I now know wholeheartedly is that I am destined to be a mother and through reading this book I have no doubt in my mind that this Promised Miracle will happen for me too, just as it did for Cheree.

Reading her testimony is moving, this book is not just ideas but deep grounded truth and empowerment, a catalyst and guided process of healing - this book will create generations of babies to come, this is what I truly believe.

Kiah Woodall
Healer & Counsellor

Disclaimer: This book shares spiritual insights, biblical teachings, and personal testimony drawn from my faith journey with Jesus. While I offer tools rooted in God's Word and therapeutic principles, this book is not intended to replace individualised medical advice, diagnosis, or treatment from healthcare professionals.

The guidance provided is meant to nurture your faith and spiritual wellbeing as you believe for the blessing of motherhood. For any health or medical concerns, please consult with a qualified healthcare provider.

Please note that individual experiences may vary, and the author and publisher encourage you to use discernment as you apply these tools in your life.

"Now Faith is the confidence in what we hope for and
assurance of things we do not see"
Hebrews 11:1

CONTENTS

About the Author

Miracle Mother, Faith Guide

Cheree is a devoted mother to her miracle son Noah, born at 41, after years of barrenness. A prophetic pioneer, intercessor & counsellor from Queensland, Australia, she walks in the authority of her testimony—transformed from hopelessness to overflowing joy.

Cheree is an author, a mother to the nations and a faithful lover of Jesus and is passionate about the supernatural, healing, deliverance and the spiritual realm.

Cheree's heart is to encourage, equip and empower women to walk into their motherhood desires. As a prophetic voice, intercessor, pioneer and watchman, she loves seeing people break free from past bondage into their God-given destiny.

Through *A Mother's Heart*, she imparts the spiritual activations, faith filled declarations, and mind-renewal tools that prepared her womb and heart for God's promise—awakening your preparation season for supernatural breakthrough.

Dedication

To every woman believing and hoping for a baby,
For every journey of waiting and trusting in God's perfect timing,
My prayer for you is that God will bless you with the desires of
your heart through these pages, just as He has blessed me.

To my beautiful miracle son, Noah,
You are the desires of my heart,
A precious gift from the Lord,
A testament to His faithfulness and abundant grace.

You are a living testimony of God's love and faithfulness—
A promise fulfilled through a thousand generations,
A shining example of the God who never forgets His children.

From the moment I first prayed for you,
to the day I held you in my arms,
You have filled my life with joy, hope, love and purpose.
This book is for you.

Noah, May your life always remind us of God's promises,
For your very existence is a promise of His steadfast love

And His blessings to a thousand generations
To those who love Him and keep His commandments.

I love you son,
With all my love,
Mum xx

Children are a gift from the Lord;
they are a reward from him.
Psalms 127:3

Acknowledgments

To our beautiful Father God in Heaven—without whom I would not be a Mother to my precious son, Noah. I honour You and thank You with all my heart for Your love, grace, goodness, faithfulness, and the gift of life. Thank you for being a good good Father.

To my spiritual parents, Steve and Wendy Backlund, and the Igniting Hope team, thank you for sparking the light within me and making this book possible. I am deeply grateful for your profound wisdom and revelations, which have transformed my journey with Jesus that will ripple through the generations. Thank you for believing in me.

Thank You

To my beautiful sisters in Christ— Marianne Petersen, Wendy Nix, Ricka Chong, and Thelma Parker—your love, support, and encouragement have carried me through this journey and lifted me up.

A special thank you to Marianne and Wendy, whose tireless editing wove grace into every page of this book. You held my words with such care, sharpening my testimony while lifting my spirit through your support and encouragement. I am so grateful for your faithful hearts.

A heartfelt honour to my beautiful family, You all shine so brightly. Noah and I love you all dearly.

To my church family—thank you for believing in me, cheering me on, and creating a joyful & loving place for me to grow in my walk with God.

Shani, thank you for your love and support during the season these pages were written. You are woven into my healing story.

I am so grateful for my family.

Introduction

I asked the Lord a question that changed everything:
"Lord, why can't I have a baby?"

This simple yet profound question marked the very beginning of my preparation season—a sacred time of transformation, healing, and hope, which eventually led to the birth of my beautiful son, Noah. Looking back, I realise how much hindsight reveals what foresight could not yet see. Midway through that season, God gently revealed to me that He was at work, tearing down lies, planting His truth deep within my spirit, healing my heart and womb, and preparing me for a miracle and a promise that was already on the way.

God is a God of families, and His love for your family is written throughout Scripture in stories of faith, covenant, and promise. Two of the most beautiful assurances is found in the following scriptures.

"Know therefore that the Lord your God is God; he is the faithful God, keeping his covenant of love to a thousand generations of those who love him and keep his commandments." Deuteronomy 7:9

May the Lord God of your fathers make you a thousand times more numerous than you are, and bless you as He has promised you. Deuteronomy 1:11

This promise of faithfulness and generational blessing is both powerful and personal. First, God is a faithful and loyal God—He will do exactly what He says He will do. His Word never returns empty or void but accomplishes everything He sends it out to do (Isaiah 55:11). Second, He promises to pour out His unfailing love not only on you but also on a thousand generations of your family as you love Him and follow His ways.

The heart of this promise speaks into family, legacy and divine destiny. God's love and blessing extend far beyond your own life, it includes children and their children to a thousand generations. This promise is for you—right now, in this very season. Remember the truth in Numbers 23:19, *"God is not human, that he should lie, not a human being, that he should change his mind."* You can trust Him fully.

Grab hold of this promise and speak it over yourself, your husband and your family daily. The Bible instructs us to *"call those things that be not as though they were"* (Romans 4:17, KJV). Speak God's promises as if they are already your reality because they are true in His timing and perfect will. When fear or weariness knocks at your door, speak faith-filled words of life and hope. Let your words declare the victory that is yours in Christ.

If your heart's deepest desire is to be a mother, then this book is an invitation into God's promise and purpose for your life. I wrote this book for you because I believe with all my heart that God is ready to bless you with a child—a beautiful baby born out of His perfect timing and love.

Revelation 19:10 declares that the testimony of Jesus is the spirit of prophecy, and this truth powerfully activates my testimony of Jesus healing my womb and blessing me with my son which prophesies breakthrough directly into your life right now.

When we experience victory in one area, it becomes a prophetic promise for others. I truly believe my testimony carries this Spirit-led power to set you free, declaring over your desire for a baby: supernatural breakthrough fills your journey through Jesus Christ.

James 1:12 reminds us that the one who overcomes will receive the crown of life, and a crown symbolises authority. I have overcome in the area of bearing a child, and I want to impart to you that this same authority and victory belong to you.

You may be in a season of preparation, as I once was, when God is aligning every detail of your life for this miracle. Psalm 37:4 encourages us: *'Take delight in the Lord, and He will give you the desires of your heart.'*

Within the pages of this book, I will share my personal testimony—the conversations I had with God, the spiritual tools and scriptures that encouraged me, and the faith-filled steps that sustained me through the waiting and preparing. This season calls for intention: you are not alone—all of heaven stands with you. It is a pathway to blessings, healing, and new life.

If you are reading this now, it is no coincidence. I believe this is the beginning of your own preparation season. You have been called to hope, to believe, and to expect God's promises to manifest. So, get excited! Attach your faith to His Word. Fill your heart with hope and joy. Know beyond any doubt that God's promises for you include children—joy-filled, He will bring your dreams to birth.

When God laid this book on my heart, He also shared a promise—thousands of babies will come into this world because of what He will do through these pages. All Glory belongs to Him alone.

If God did it for me, He can surely do it for you. My prayer for you is that you cling passionately to faith, hope, and love as God leads you on a beautiful, redemptive journey toward the birth of your precious baby.

May this testimony break chains, release faith, and bring miracles to you and your family.

Blessings and love,
Cheree xx

Chapter 1

From Longing to Believing:
Healing the Heart's Desire

Take delight in the LORD, and he will give you the desires of your heart.
— Psalms *37:4*

This scripture was one of the two key verses I clung to during my preparation season for my beautiful son, Noah. For many years, my heart longed for a baby, but before I surrendered my life to Jesus, I had accepted the painful idea that I might never become a mother. I reasoned that having nieces and nephews was enough and children would never become a realty for me. But God had other plans—plans that would far exceed what I imagined.

I was 39 when I gave my heart fully to Jesus. Before that, I had doubted His existence and questioned if God was real. Then, in a moment I now recognise as supernatural, God healed me from the torment of my childhood traumas. It was a freedom I had never experienced before—a breakthrough that ignited a deep desire within me to know more about what I initially described to myself as a "phenomena", the God who had set me free. This was the beginning of a wonderful relationship with Jesus, the foundation of my preparation season to become a Mother.

My new family of believers never pressured me; instead, they loved me and let Jesus do the transforming work. Over the following weeks, the Lord began unraveling the lies I had believed about myself and the mother He had created me to be. I had resigned myself to never becoming a mother—a lie forged from fear, doubt, and pain.

I believed I was too old, too broken, or that adding a baby to this chaotic world was unwise. For too long, my mind was filled with the enemy's lies. I lost sight of God's promises and as a new believer, I did not yet realise I had a choice—to accept these lies or to embrace truth.

I know firsthand the discouragement that fills a woman's heart when her desire to have a baby seems to remain unfulfilled. Sometimes, you feel overlooked by God, as if He doesn't see your pain.

During these seasons, the enemy whispers lies that replay in your mind like echoes: "Maybe I am too old to be a mother," "Maybe I am not meant to have children," or "I'm better off just being an auntie—I can hand the baby back" and I settled with a belief that I was a career woman and being a mother was now becoming far from my sight. These lies seek to steal your hope and steal your joy.

A few weeks after asking the Lord, "Why can't I conceive?", I attended a deliverance and healing workshop where the facilitator spoke about the vagabond spirit—a spirit described in Genesis 4:12:

"When you work the ground, it will no longer yield its crops for you. You will be a restless wanderer on the earth."

This spirit represents rootlessness, instability, and a sense of not belonging—manifesting as feeling lost and cut off from God's blessings. My spirit leaped.

During the workshop, God gave me a revelation: *"The vagabond spirit is attached to your womb and making you infertile."* I was overwhelmed with excitement! This was it, this makes sense", I thought because for years I had felt unsettled and disconnected, searching for peace through different means.

Prior to giving my heart to the Lord, I followed New Age practices for 20 years before my supernatural encounter with God. At the time of this encounter, I was actually in the middle of learning reiki. Not long after I met Jesus, I called the reiki teacher and said to her, "I've found Jesus, and He is the One you are searching for too."

For all those years, I was desperately searching for peace from the torment of my childhood trauma. I tried all kinds of new age practices, but the peace they gave was a counterfeit of God's peace, it was temporary and never lasting, and it always left me longing for more.

I genuinely had no idea I was partnering with the kingdom of darkness through these practices—my heart was simply searching for love, peace, and joy. I didn't know it at the time but I was searching for Jesus.

Soon after this revelation, I praised God fervently, thanking Him for His faithfulness and this divine insight. Why, because the same spirit that raised Jesus from the dead was the same spirit that would bring life to my womb. I prayed, *"Lord, how do You want to break this vagabond spirit from my womb? What should I do next?"* I surrendered everything with faith, filled with hope for a new chapter. I knew God was going to heal my womb and bless me with a child.

This was the beginning of my preparation season. Over the next 12 months God began to do a a deep work in me. He began with revealing lies I was believing and teaching me how to surrender those lies and replace them with His truth from His word.

Little did I know that I was renewing my mind with lies and fears about being a Mother for many years which became the truth for me. The Lord took me through a heart healing journey, unpacking negative emotional strongholds that were keeping me stuck in the lies and He began replacing them with his truth.

Whilst in my preparation season, the Lord healed my heart and set me free from trauma that plagued me since my childhood. He was so loving and gentle and I fell deeply in love with Jesus daily.

At the end of my preparation season, while volunteering in a prayer ministry, I joined a five-day fast. During this fast, the Lord impressed on my spirit: *"It is during this fast that I will heal your womb."* Though inexperienced with fasting, I sought wise counsel and committed myself wholeheartedly, hopeful and expectant of God's work. It was January 2015.

On the fifth day, when the prayer team gathered to pray for one another, I instantly knew it was my time. When invited, I raised my hand and said, "Please pray for me. The Lord revealed to me that a vagabond spirit is attached to my womb, making me infertile."

The team prayed over me with faith and authority. It was a powerful and unforgettable moment of deliverance.

Six weeks later, I became pregnant with my beautiful son, Noah—a living testament to God's power to restore, heal, and bring fruitfulness from barrenness. The chains of that wandering spirit were broken, and true freedom was unlocked.

My testimony is a reminder that God breaks every curse, replaces wandering with belonging, and ushers in new life. After discovering my pregnancy, I shared the news with trusted prayer warriors to cover both me and my baby in prayer. Many women are told to keep pregnancies a secret for the first three months "just in case." But I knew that this was a lie from the enemy—a whisper of fear I refused to accept.

God had knitted my baby in my womb (Psalm 139:13-14) and declared my child fearfully and wonderfully made. I shared my pregnancy news with close friends and family and they were all just as happy and excited as I was and their prayers covered Noah and I during my pregnancy. I was 41 years old when Noah was born on the 16th October 2015.

No matter what lies the enemy or the world has whispered over your heart, this book will help you replace them with God's truth. His Word is a sword, sharper than the sharpest two-edged blade, cutting through bondage and fear (Hebrews 4:12). God is not a man that He should lie (Numbers 23:19), and Jesus Christ is the same yesterday, today, and forever (Hebrews 13:8).

GOD'S PROMISES TO WOMEN
LONGING FOR CHILDREN

God desires to bless you with a family, and His Word affirms this repeatedly—regardless of your age or circumstances. Let me say that again: regardless of your age or circumstances, so If you believed a lie that you are to old to have children let's break this lie right now in Jesus name.

Psalm 113:9 declares:
"He gives the barren woman a home, making her the joyous mother of children. Praise the Lord!"

This verse powerfully declares God's ability to turn barrenness into joyful motherhood. It doesn't limit this promise to young women alone—you don't have to settle for being an aunt or spiritual mother (not that there's anything wrong with these beautiful callings). God has promised you your own baby. This promise is real, tangible, and for you, no matter your age.

Consider Sarah, who was ninety years old (Genesis 21:1-2):
"The Lord visited Sarah as He had said, and the Lord did to Sarah as He had promised. Sarah conceived and bore Abraham a son."
God's promise was fulfilled despite human impossibility.

Similarly, in Luke 1:36, the angel Gabriel tells Mary:
"Even Elizabeth your relative is going to have a child in her old age, and she who was said to be barren is in her sixth month."
This is a powerful testimony to God's supernatural power to bring life where it seems impossible.

Does this excite you? Does it fill you with hope? Stir up excitement and joy with in you because God's plans and timing are perfect—they transcend age, status, or nationality. For me, it seemed impossible because of my age and my circumstances, but God had supernatural plans.

When I asked the Lord, "Why can't I have children?", He didn't answer instantly. Instead, He invited me into faith, assuring me revelation would come in His perfect time. I surrendered and trusted completely.

Hebrews 11:1 became my anchor:
"Now faith is the confidence in what we hope for and assurance about what we do not see." Notice the word *Now*. This is faith to walk in TODAY— not tomorrow, not next week, but faith for this very moment.

Every time I prayed about having a baby, I attached *Now Faith* to my prayers. I declared, *"Lord, thank You that I now receive revelation in my preparation season, I trust You, I love You, and I surrender this to You."* I believed that without a shadow of a doubt that God would answer my prayers.

Steve Backlund defines faith as believing firmly that God's promises and your past prayers are at work in your life. The Greek word *pistis* means trust, conviction, and confidence in God's promises— far beyond intellectual agreement, involving deep personal trust and reliance on God.

Faith means you trust God's unseen promises and live in alignment with His Word being fully convinced that God will answer your prayers and fulfil his promise. In Hebrew 4:21, it says Abraham was fully convinced that God's is able to what He promises, and that promise was for him and Sarah to have a baby.

In the next chapter, we will unpack this Scripture in greater detail, because *Now Faith* will be a key to your preparation season.

Friends, I am so excited for you. This is your season. Let's begin this miracle journey!

ACTIVATION

Spend quiet time soaking in the Lord's presence.

Ask the Lord:
"Why can't I fall pregnant?"
"What do I need to believe to have a baby"?

Surrender these question's fully to Him. Trust in His perfect timing and revelation. Start praising Him in advance for the wisdom and truth you will receive. When your mind returns to this prayer, speak with *Now Faith*:

"Father, thank You for bringing wisdom and revelation. I trust You, I love You, and I surrender this desire to You, Jesus."

SURRENDERING LIES

Breathe deeply in God's presence again.

Ask the Lord, *"Are there any lies I am believing about having a baby?"* Write down any words or feelings He brings to your heart. Common lies might be: *"I am too old,"* or *"I am not meant to be a mother."*

Pray this aloud and declare:

"Lord, I repent of believing the lie that I am too old to have children. I renounce this lie and surrender it to You, Jesus. I choose Your truth and promises as my foundation."

DECLARATIONS OF FAITH

- The Lord is faithful and answers my prayers.

- I receive a constant flow of wisdom and revelation from the Lord.

- God's promises and my past prayers are working in my life, my family's life, and my circumstances.

- I embrace *Now Faith* and trust God's timing for my miracle.

- I declare healing, fruitfulness, and blessing over my womb.

- I am a beloved daughter of God, and His love surrounds me and my baby.

DAILY REFLECTION PROMPTS

- How am I feeling today about my journey toward motherhood?

- What lies or fears did I notice creeping into my thoughts?

- What truth from God's Word can I declare over myself today?

- How did I experience or recognise God's presence or peace today?

- What Scriptures or prayers ministered to my heart today?

DAILY PRAYER STARTERS

- "Lord, help me trust You fully today and lean not on my own understanding (Proverbs 3:5)."

- "Father God, reveal any lies I am believing and help me surrender them to You."

- "Jesus, I ask for Your healing power to flow through my heart and womb."

- "Holy Spirit, fill me with wisdom, faith, hope and peace as I wait on God's perfect timing."

- "Thank You, Lord, for Your faithfulness and for the promises You have spoken over me."

WEEKLY SCRIPTURE MEDITATIONS

- **Week 1:** *Proverbs 3:5-6* — Trusting God with all my heart.

- **Week 2:** *Deuteronomy 7:9* — God's covenant love for generations.

- **Week 3:** *Psalm 139:13-14* — Fearfully and wonderfully made.

- **Week 4:** *Hebrews 11:1* — Now faith for what I hope for.

Reflect on one verse each day this week. Write about how it personally encourages and strengthens you.

FAITH-FILLED DECLARATIONS

Say one or all of these declarations aloud daily, confidently and joyfully:

- "I walk in faith, embracing God's perfect timing."

- "God's promises over my life are true and unstoppable."

- "I release every lie and declare I am worthy and loved."

- "My womb is healed, fertile, and fertile for new life."

- "I am a daughter of the King, prepared for motherhood."

- "Now faith fills my heart and guides my steps."

PRACTICAL ACTIVATION IDEAS

- Create a "Faith Jar": Write prayers, declarations, and things you are thankful for on slips of paper and place them in a jar. Read them when you need encouragement.

- Engage in daily quiet time with God—set aside 10-15 minutes for Scripture, prayer, and listening.

- Connect weekly with a trusted prayer partner or group to share your journey and receive support.

- Use creative expression: draw, journal, or sing your prayers and hopes, inviting God into your healing.

- Celebrate small victories and answered prayers, no matter how tiny—they are steps forward. Celebrate progress over perfection.

Embrace this truth with confidence, and be ready to receive the supernatural blessings He has prepared for you.

The next chapter invites you to walk daily in faith and hope as God brings your heart's desires to life. Know that you are deeply loved, carefully prepared, and wonderfully made for this sacred journey.

Chapter 2

Now Faith

*"Now faith is the confidence of what we hope for and
assurance of things we cannot see"* — Hebrews 11:1

Hebrews 11:1 is foundational for understanding what faith truly is, especially when it comes to believing for a child. This verse invites you into a deep, steadfast trust—a trust that holds fast to hope even when the visible evidence is absent. When you hope for a baby, faith requires that you walk through uncertainty with confidence, confident that God's promise is certain, though its fulfilment may still be unseen.

I am going to unpack Hebrews 11:1 in terms of believing for a baby. Hebrews 11:1 says, *"Now faith is the confidence of what we hope for and assurance of things we cannot see."* I love unpacking the meaning of words, To fully grasp this, it helps to explore the original Hebrew and Greek terms behind the word *faith.* let's look at faith in Hebrew, Greek, and English.

The Hebrew word for faith is הָאֱמוּנָה (**emunah**), which means firmness, steadfastness, loyalty, and a trust that leads to faithful action and endurance. It is not just a mental agreement but an active reliance on God's promises.

Emunah is rooted in loyalty and steadfastness; it is a covenantal trust that brings a person into a committed relationship with God where their actions reflect their inner conviction. It means holding tight to what God has said, even when the circumstances seem overwhelming or impossible.

The Greek word is **πίστις (pistis)**, meaning conviction, firm persuasion, trust, and reliance on God's character and promises. Pistis focuses on a personal trust in God grounded in His faithfulness and power.

It is more than intellectual assent; it is confidence that results in actual reliance and dependent obedience. In the New Testament, pistis is often paired with works (James 2:22), showing that true faith compels action, a faith consistent with believing God's promises and living accordingly.

In English, faith is generally defined as trust, belief, or confidence, but biblically it means assurance of what we hope for, combined with acting on God's promises. It requires steadfastness and confidence in the invisible, a boldness to believe even before seeing the evidence. These dimensions together show that biblical faith is not mere belief but a steady, enduring relationship with God involving trust and obedience.

Steadfast assurance is critical in the journey of believing for a baby. This faith speaks into the confident expectation that God will bless you with a child, despite what the world may say. The very fact you are reading this book shows your desire and faith to believe for a baby.

Faith means trusting God—not shrinking back—and believing that God can and will fulfil His promise to you. It is refusing to waver and choosing daily to speak life over your womb, your future, and your hope.

My legacy scripture is Deuteronomy 7:9, which says:

"Know therefore that the Lord your God is God; he is the faithful God, keeping his covenant of love to a thousand generations of those who love him and keep his commandments."

This verse assures us that God is unfailing in His promises and shows steadfast love to those who belong to Him—this promise is for you and your husband. It reminds us that God's faithfulness spans beyond ourselves to future generations. His love is long-lasting, covenantal, and active. He rewards faithfulness with continued blessing, opening the door for generational miracles and fruitfulness.

Galatians 3:29 echoes this hope, saying,

"If you belong to Christ, then you are Abraham's seed, and heirs according to the promise."

God promised Abraham descendants as numerous as the stars in the sky—a promise that extends to us today. Be encouraged; this promise is powerful and is for you. Each generation is an inheritor of God's covenantal blessings and faithfulness. Your faith links you to this great cloud of witnesses who trusted God's promises even when they were unseen.

In Genesis 1:27, God blessed Adam & Eve and says to them, *"Be fruitful & multiply"*. This is a prophetic word for you and your husband today. God has blessed you both and He is speaking over you, *"Be fruitful & multiply"*.

Numbers 23:19 declares,

"God is not a man, that He should lie, nor a son of man, that He should change His mind. Does He speak and not act? Does He promise and not fulfil?"

So, we can boldly call forth God's promises of blessing, fruitfulness & multiplication trusting that His Word never returns void. Though doubt and fear may creep in—as they did for me—God's faithfulness overcomes every lie.

We must remember that every promise God makes is yes and amen (2 Corinthians 1:20). When God promises a baby, He does not hesitate or falter; His Word will accomplish all He purposes.

Let this truth sink deep: God keeps every promise. When He promises children, His Word stands firm. Doubt may try to shake you, but God's faithfulness is a firm rock you can trust on every side.

Paul echoes this in 2 Corinthians 1:20:

"For no matter how many promises God has made, they are 'Yes' in Christ. And so through him the 'Amen' is spoken by us to the glory of God."

THE JOURNEY OF FAITH IN MOTHERHOOD

As you journey toward motherhood, steadfast faith becomes crucial. Faith is not passive or wishful thinking; it is confident expectation—a knowing deep within that God will bless you with a child despite what doctors say or what circumstances seem to dictate. The mere fact that you hold this book and desire to believe for a baby reflects your brave choice to trust God amid uncertainty.

You refuse to shrink back or surrender to despair. Every day, you speak life over your womb, your future, and your hopes. Just as Abraham *"believed God, and it was credited to him as righteousness"* (Romans 4:3), you are called to trust and rely on God's promises for your life's next chapter.

GOD'S DELIGHT IN BLESSING CHILDREN

Children are a precious heritage and a reward from the Lord:

"Behold, children are a heritage from the Lord, the fruit of the womb a reward."
— Psalm 127:3

Hannah's prayerful longing was answered just as she prayed:

"For this child I prayed, and the Lord has granted me what I asked of Him."
— 1 Samuel 1:27

God's promises delight in blessing the fruit of your womb:

"He will bless the fruit of your womb."
— Deuteronomy 7:13

His power brings life and brings to birth what He ordains:

"Shall I bring to the point of birth and not give delivery? says the Lord."
— Isaiah 66:9

Such words feed your hope even when the odds seem stacked. My son Noah was born when I was 41, a time the world called "geriatric motherhood." But remember we are in this world but we, as faith filled sincere believers, are not of it. God's timing was perfect—His promises never fail.

HOLDING FAST IN THE WAITING

The waiting can feel unbearable at times. I know the sorrow of watching others build families while you quietly carry heartbreak. You are genuinely happy for those around you, yet there remains that deep longing to start your own family — a silent ache that weighs on the heart.

Proverbs 13:12 says, *"Hope deferred makes the heart sick, but a longing fulfilled is a tree of life."* When the hope of a child feels delayed, the heart can grow weary. But when God fulfils that longing, it becomes a *tree of life* — a source of joy, fruitfulness, and generational blessing. Your motherhood will not just bless you; it will be a generational breakthrough that releases hope and healing, as God's promises bloom within your family.

Romans 4:17 reminds us that God *"calls into being things that do not exist."* This truth gives you the courage to speak life and fertility over your womb and your dreams — even before they become visible. Luke 1:45 declares, *"Blessed is she who has believed that the Lord would fulfil His promises to her."* What a powerful assurance from the Lord; we will go deeper into this in Chapter 4.

Faith is active trust in what cannot yet be seen (2 Corinthians 5:7). It holds steady in uncertainty and anchors hope in God's nature. As Romans 10:17 says, *"Faith comes by hearing, and hearing through the word of Christ."* Let God's Word be your daily nourishment, strengthening your faith and reminding you that you are His beloved daughter, chosen to receive His promises.

Reflecting on years of heartache and hopelessness, I remember feeling like a failure as others around me had children. As Solomon wrote, *"Hope deferred makes the heart sick,"* and I understood that deeply. But when God fulfils that longing, it truly becomes a *tree of life* — reviving the soul, bringing healing, and creating a legacy that blesses generations. This is more than a personal victory; it is a testament to God's goodness and faithfulness.

Romans 4:17 again reminds us that God *"calls into being things that do not exist."* Speaking life through faith activates expectation. Faith is not wishful thinking — it is confidence that what God said, He will do. To walk by faith, not by sight (2 Corinthians 5:7), is to trust His timing and goodness completely, knowing that every delay still carries purpose in preparing you for His promise.

SCIENTIFIC INSIGHTS ON FAITH, MINDSET, AND FERTILITY

Modern medicine confirms Scripture—the deep connection between your heart and womb. High stress disrupts hormones essential for ovulation and fertility (American Society for Reproductive Medicine, 2022), while faith, prayer, and meditation lower stress and restore balance, enhancing conception chances (Journal of Psychosomatic Obstetrics & Gynecology, 2020). Healing your heart creates fertile ground—emotionally, spiritually, and physically—for God's miracle.

This chapter invites you to walk daily in faith and hope as God fulfils your deepest desires. Know you are deeply loved, carefully prepared, and wonderfully made for this sacred journey. Embrace this truth confidently, ready to receive His supernatural blessings.

ACTIVATION: CULTIVATING NOW FAITH

1. Daily Word Immersion
Commit to reading faith-filled scriptures such as Hebrews 11, Romans 4, Galatians 3, Psalm 127. Write down the verse that stirs your heart most each day and meditate on it through prayer.

2. Confident Declarations
Speak these aloud every day:

- "My faith is unwavering and rooted in the promises of God."
- "I declare life and blessing over my womb and future children."
- "God's timing is perfect, and I rejoice in His plan."
- "I am heir to Abraham's promise and a daughter of destiny."
- "Now faith fills my heart and leads my steps daily."

3. Journaling Prompts
Reflect on these:

- What fears or doubts can I surrender today?

- How has God been faithful in my past?

- How will I act in faith despite not yet seeing the outcome?

4. Build a Promise Board

Collect key scriptures, prayers, and affirmations on a physical or digital board to visualise daily. Use it as a source of encouragement.

5. Prayer Partnerships

Find a trusted prayer partner or group who will support and remind you of God's truths during the journey.

DECLARATIONS OF FAITH

- "I declare my faith is strong and immovable, built on God's sure Word."

- "By faith, I release blessing and fruitfulness over my womb."

- "I wait patiently, trusting God's perfect timing and promises."

- "God's covenant love surrounds me and my future family."

- "I am empowered and joyful as I walk this faith-filled path."

Declarations:

- "I declare that my faith is steadfast and confident in the promises of God. I am assured of the fruitfulness He has prepared for me, even what I cannot yet see."

- "By faith, I speak life and blessing over my womb. I trust that God's promise will be fulfilled, and I receive His hope, joy, and peace as I wait patiently for His perfect timing."

CLOSING WORDS

Faith is one of your key's to unlocking God's promises for your life. Even when the path seems unclear, trust the One who calls into existence what does not yet exist. God's faithfulness transcends age, circumstance, and time.

You are surrounded by a great cloud of witnesses—women of faith who climbed their mountains and trusted their promises until they saw miracles. Your motherhood journey is sacred, divinely beautiful, and part of God's grand story.

Hold tight to your promise and your hope. Let your faith grow every day, anchored in Scripture and declarations of life. *Now faith* is your path forward.

Chapter 3

Hope

"Now may the God of hope fill you with all joy and peace in believing, that you may abound in hope by the power of the Holy Spirit."
— Romans 15:13

The ache of not having my own baby and starting my own family was inside of me as I watched others around me start families, my longing growing heavier with each passing day. I remember times when the heaviness felt unbearable, the silence of unmet dreams pressing in. For my own peace of mind I created fear based lies that became beliefs for me concluding that children were not meant for me or I am happy just being the Aunty and then I could hand the child back.

I also remember a time I was declaring lies over myself that I am a career woman, I have no time for children. When I look back in that time of my life, I realised that for me. I created these lies because I had hope deferred. I didn't know at the time that I was renewing my mind with lies about myself that pushed my desires of having a baby further and further away from me, the pain of not having my own child was unbearable.

Yet, through God's gentle grace, my understanding began to shift. Real hope, biblically founded and life-giving, which is far beyond mere wishful thinking. It is a powerful anchor, a confident expectation rooted in the unwavering promises of God. It is not just a passive longing; it is an overflowing, joyful expectation that good is coming into your life—because God is faithful.

Romans 15:13 offers a beautiful prayer over us, saying, *"Now may the God of hope fill you with all joy and peace in believing, that you may abound in hope by the power of the Holy Spirit."* This verse stirs my soul because it reminds me that hope is a gift from God—a living force that fills us with joy and peace, not merely emotions that rise and fall with circumstance. It is a hope that sustains deeply, nurtures patiently, and overflows abundantly through the empowerment of the Holy Spirit.

I love Steve Backlund's definition of Hope, He says, "Hope is believing the future will be better than the present and you have the power to help make it so.". All my life I believed a lie that hope was wishful thinking, something that was out of reach, unattainable. Gods word however, gives us a richer understanding. Hope is a confident expectation, a firm assurance, and a bold trust anchored in God's faithfulness and His never-failing promises.

Hebrews 6:19 tells us, *"We have this hope as an anchor for the soul, firm and secure."* This verse speaks powerfully to me—hope is not tentative or uncertain; it steadies the soul amid storms, holding us fast when all around seems to shake. It is an active trust that carries us through long seasons of waiting, pushing us forward even when the evidence hasn't yet appeared, and our desires feel dormant.

Hope is partnered deeply with faith. It is the authority and partnership God grants us through faith — the power to speak life, shape circumstances, and co-labor with Him to bring promises into reality. This dynamic interplay between hope and faith is not passive or disconnected; it is a powerful force that is deeply life-transforming.

I reflect often on the truth that I spoke over myself in my preparation season, every hopeful word I speak over my womb, my body, my family, and my future is stepping into the power God has given me. Proverbs 18:21 declares, *"Death and life are in the power of the tongue, and those who love it will eat its fruits."*

These words remind me daily to choose life—words that bring hope and faith to light, that push back against despair and fear. Isaiah 55:11 reassures us that God's word never returns void but always accomplishes His purposes, reminding us that when hope is anchored in God's promises, it awakens divine power and fruitfulness.

I often think of Romans 15:13 again: *"May the God of hope fill you with all joy and peace as you trust in Him, so that you may overflow with hope by the power of the Holy Spirit."* This joy and peace are not mere feelings but supernatural gifts given to sustain us in the waiting seasons. When you are feeling overwhelmed or tempted to doubt, remember this promise and invite the Holy Spirit to fill you, knowing that hope is meant to overflow—even before the miracle you long for arrives.

Jesus described hope's power in John 14:12 when He said, *"Truly, truly, I say to you, whoever believes in me will also do the works that I do; and greater works than these will he do, because I am going to the Father."* Even though Jesus did not have children, His promise extends to all of us—to partner with God in the miraculous, to participate in life-giving works, and to walk in the fullness of God's promises.

Your hope is part of this greater work; it opens the door to miracles that surpass human understanding and reveals God's power at work in and through you. Lean heavily on God's covenant promises, especially knowing that He honours lineage and faithfulness.

Deuteronomy 7:9 says, *"Know therefore that the Lord your God is God; He is the faithful God, keeping His covenant of love to a thousand generations of those who love Him and keep His commandments."* This reminds us that your hope for a family is not only personal but generational—a blessing that flows far beyond your lifetime, touching children, grandchildren, and many generations beyond.

Psalm 127:3 calls children *"a heritage from the Lord, the fruit of the womb a reward."* Hannah's heartfelt prayer resonated with my own longing during my preparation season: "For this child I prayed, and the Lord has granted me what I asked of Him" (1 Samuel 1:27). These scriptures confirm God's delight in expanding families and blessing the fruit of our wombs.

Looking back, there were moments when hope felt an impossible dream. I had more faith in hope deferred—waiting, delayed fulfilment—than in hope itself. Yet, Proverbs 13:12 shines like a lamp in the darkness: *"Hope deferred makes the heart sick, but a longing fulfilled is a tree of life."* Even when the waiting felt endless, these words encouraged me. Waiting is not wasted time; it is fertile ground where faith and hope take root, planting seeds that will blossom into a tree of life—a legacy of nourishment and blessing for generations.

Romans 4:17 reminds us that God "calls into being things that do not exist." This truth invites you to boldly speak life over your womb and dreams even before physical evidence appears. Luke 1:45 blesses the woman who believes: *"Blessed is she who has believed that the Lord would fulfil His promises to her."* Let this verse anchor your heart in faith as you walk by faith, not by sight (2 Corinthians 5:7), trusting that God's timing and plans are perfect, even when the natural world seems silent.

I have come to understand that hope is like a spiritual muscle, growing stronger the more I exercise it through prayer, declaration, and trust. Romans 5:3-5 tells us that suffering produces perseverance; perseverance, character; and character, hope. Every trial refines hope and prepares you for the the breakthrough God has planned. This intertwining of hope and faith creates momentum, empowering us to step daily into the unseen realm with confident expectation.

Hebrews 11, known as the faith chapter, features countless heroes who walked by hope and faith toward impossible promises. Their journey is inspiring—a journey where each hopeful step is a declaration that your miracle is near. Romans 4:20-21 beautiful encapsulates Abrahams unwavering faith in God, he knew that God would come good on His promises for a heir for him and Sarah.

Love, too, plays a vital role in keeping hope alive. It softens our hearts, drives out fear, and sustains the deepest longings of our soul. Without love, hope falters; but with God's perfect love protecting and guiding you through your preparation season, your hope grows steadfast.

As 1 Corinthians 13 reminds us, *"Now these three remain: faith, hope, and love. But the greatest of these is love."* The divine love we hold onto surrounds you with hope, shielding it from weariness and doubt, nurturing a fierce confidence that what you wait for is on its way.

Living with joy fuelled by hope has transformed my daily walk. Hope is not just for the future—it is a celebration today. I intentionally choose joy, celebrate every sign of progress, and welcome peace even in the waiting. Sarah's story, laughing at God's promise in old age and later holding Isaac, reminds me that God's timing is never wrong, and His miracles unfold in perfect season.

Hope is a divine gift, a sacred promise that can strengthen you daily. Wendy Backlund says that our imagination is the womb of our faith, this is such a powerful revelation, couple this revelation with hope and begin to imagine the promises of God in your life, visualise yourself holding your child and give thanks for the miracle before it fully appears.

Each morning I declare, *"Today I choose hope. I take hold of God's promises and speak life into my future."* This prayer anchors my heart when negativity whispers. You can remind yourself that hope is a confident expectation upon the faithfulness of God. Embrace this hope daily knowing that God's ways are higher than yours, and

His promises stand firm knowing your future is better than the present and you have the power to help make it so.

God's promises and equips us to press forward through every season, confidently declaring blessing over our lives and the futures we long for. The waiting times often feel like desert places—dryness, loneliness, and longing seemingly unfulfilled. watching others embrace motherhood while you wait can induce heartbreak and despair. Proverbs 13:12 captures this well:

"Hope deferred makes the heart sick, but a longing fulfilled is a tree of life."

When God finally answers, hope blossoms into a *tree of life*—deeply nourishing your family's future. Your motherhood journey becomes more than personal joy; it is a generational breakthrough. Let me share this scripture with you again, romans 4:17 reminds us God *"calls into being things that do not exist."* God enables you to speak into your womb and dreams confidently, moving beyond the visible.

SCIENCE MEETS SCRIPTURE: HOPE, MINDSET, AND HEALING

Research increasingly affirms hope's healing power. According to the American Psychological Association (2018), hope correlates with better health outcomes, faster recovery, and greater emotional resilience. Hope energises the nervous system and boosts the immune system.

PRACTICAL REFLECTIONS ON HOPE'S POWER

Each morning as you rise, breathe in this truth: you are an active participant in your miracle. You have the authority, given by God, to shape your journey through hope-filled words and faith. Declare over yourself:

"Today I choose hope. I take hold of God's promises and speak life into my future."

Use hope as a compass that steers your thoughts and actions. When negativity or doubt whispers, remind yourself that *hope is a confident expectation* anchored in God's faithfulness.

Remember Sarah, who laughed at the promise of a baby in old age but whose hope eventually birthed Isaac (Genesis 21). Sarah's story reminds us hope can stretch beyond human understanding into the realm of divine possibility. It encourages you to hold on when circumstances seem illogical—because God's ways are higher.

PRACTICAL HOPE-BUILDING ACTIVATIONS

1. **Scripture Meditation**
   Commit to daily reading and meditating on scripture verses that build hope and faith. Use a journal to capture insights and prayers. Suggested passages:

- Hebrews 6:19

- Romans 15:13

- Psalm 130:5-6

- Jeremiah 29:11

- Lamentations 3:22-24

- Romans 4:17

- Luke 1:45

- Proverbs 13:12

2. Hope Declarations

Speak these powerful declarations aloud mornings and evenings:

- "Hope anchors my soul and strengthens my faith daily."

- "I declare blessings and life over my womb and future."

- "God's joy and peace overflow within me as I wait."

- "Faith, hope, and love empower this sacred journey."

3. Envision Your Miracle

Spend quiet moments each day imagining holding your baby, dreaming of milestones and joyful moments. Writing or drawing these visions magnifies hope and builds emotional connection. Invite Jesus into your visions.

4. Build Your Support Circle

Connect regularly with trusted friends, mentors, or prayer groups who will uphold you, pray faithfully, and remind you of God's promises and power.

5. Gratitude Journal

Record everyday moments of hope, joy, and evidence of God's faithfulness. Reflect often on your growth and victories to strengthen hope during long waits.

ENCOURAGEMENT FOR YOUR JOURNEY

Hope is the vibrant heartbeat of your journey to motherhood. It transforms waiting into expectancy, longing into joy, and doubt into confident trust.

You are not alone. You are surrounded by a great cloud of faithful witnesses—women who kept hope alive and now celebrate their miracles. Your story joins the divine tapestry of faith, hope, and love.

Allow hope to rise within you each day, intertwined with faith and love, guiding your steps toward the wonderful fulfilment of your deepest heart desires.

Now faith, hope, and love walk hand in hand on your path forward.

FINAL REFLECTIONS

Hope is a divine gift and a powerful force—a partner that invites you into co-creation with God. It is the language of the heart that refuses to surrender, the armour shielding you from despair, and the light guiding you through darkness.

"Hope is believing the future will be better than the present and you have the power to help make it so." This is your call: to embody hope as power, faith as trust, and love as grace on your mothering journey.

Let today be your new beginning. Plant hope deeply in your soul and speak it boldly over your womb and life. Step forward confident that you move with God's promise and power. Your miracle is waiting for you to embrace it with expectant hope.

Chapter 4

She Believed

"Blessed is she who believed, for there shall be a fulfilment of those things which were told to her from the Lord." — Luke 1:45

Mary's unwavering faith in God's promise stands as a timeless beacon for all who are on a journey of hope in believing for a baby. Her story reminds us that faith blossoms into reality when it becomes fully persuaded, rooted in hope, and empowered by a confident trust in God. For those believing for a child, this kind of faith—the kind that is deeply anchored in hope and trust—is the key that unlocks the door to receiving God's promises even amidst uncertainty.

The true meaning of 'believe,' is more than just acknowledging a truth mentally. It embodies trust, confidence, and complete reliance on the faithfulness of God's Word. To believe in this way means to nurture hope actively, to align every declaration with God's promises, and to believe firmly on His promises, unwavering even when circumstances challenge that hope.

Let's look at the word — *believe.*

According to the dictionary, *believe* means to accept something as true, to have confidence or trust in a person or thing. Biblically, the word *believe* comes from the Greek word *pisteuō*, which means *to trust in, to rely upon, and to be fully convinced of* something or someone. In the Hebrew, the verb *'aman* behind believe means *to support, confirm, or make firm*, echoing the idea of placing your full weight of trust in God.

When Scripture says, *"Blessed is she who has believed,"* it speaks of Mary's faith in accepting God's word before she ever saw the promise fulfilled. To *believe* in the biblical sense is not simply to acknowledge something may happen—it means to rest completely in God's character, trusting that His promises will come to pass even when evidence seems impossible. This kind of faith brings blessing because it aligns our hearts with God's truth rather than our circumstances.

Another powerful verse on belief is Mark 9:23, where Jesus says, *"Everything is possible for one who believes."* This reminds us that believing is not passive—it is an active, ongoing truth. Believing is the opposite of doubt, do you believe God's promises for you for generational blessings? If there is hesitation than ask God, why and then surrender the lie and begin declaring the truth that you and your children are blessed to a thousand generations.

THE EXAMPLE OF ABRAHAM

Lets look at Abraham and Sarah, in Genesis 17. God changed their names, firstly from Abram to Abraham and God makes a prophetic declaration over him and says, *"I have made you a father of many nations"*. Later in the chapter, God changes his wife's name from Sarai to Sarah He then blesses her and prophetically declares over Sarah, *"She shall be a mother to the nations"*. God then says to Abraham that Sarah shall bear a son.

Abraham held onto this word from the Lord, his belief was not naive optimism but a resolute trust grounded in the very character of God—the God who neither fails nor changes. Abraham partnered with God and his belief was that he is a father to many.

Such faith refuses to partner with disappointment or impossibility. Instead, it consistently speaks life, blessing, and the fulfilment of God's promises even before they manifest visibly. I believe that this is a prophetic word for you today, all the promises of a baby that God spoke over those in the bible, He is promising you.

Believing for a baby means holding fast to this legacy of faith. It means speaking declarations of life and hope over one's body and womb, standing in the place of expectancy, and guarding the heart against the creeping lies of fear, doubt, and despair. Faith and hope are foundational pillars through which we claim the promises of God, releasing heaven's possibilities into every area where He speaks life, but first you must believe it is possible because all things are possible for the one who believes. Mark 9:23

RENEWING THE MIND TO BELIEVE

In Chapter 1, we explored an activation that invites God to reveal whether you are believing any lies about your journey to motherhood. One profound wisdom that I have learnt from my spiritual Father in my faith walk is that "every area of life without joy is an area where I have believed a lie." When discouragement sets in, it often initiates a process of renewing the mind towards hope.

God's Word declares, *"Blessed is she who believed"* (Luke 1:45). But what exactly are we believing right now? The Apostle Paul teaches us in Romans 12:2: *"Do not conform to the pattern of this world, but be transformed by the renewing of your mind."* This urging challenges us to intentionally reject the world's thought patterns and instead embrace a mindset shaped and sustained by God's Word. Are you renewing your mind daily with God's promises, or are you conforming to the lies and fear the enemy continuously whispers?

Scientific research aligns with this spiritual truth. Studies indicate that the average person has over 6,000 thoughts a day, with some claims reaching as high as 60,000. Remarkably, approximately 90% of these thoughts may be repetitive, and a significant number tend toward negativity or unhelpful patterns. This means that most people operate under a steady stream of automatic, often unconscious thinking shaped by past experiences, beliefs, and habits.

This is why Romans 12:2 is so critical—without intentional reflection and renewal, negative thought loops can go unchallenged, solidifying old mindsets and obstructing faith, hope, and change. Renewing the mind means actively deciding to surrender old thought habits—lies of fear, doubt, and hopelessness—and replacing them with God's promises and truth.

TAKING EVERY THOUGHT CAPTIVE

While we cannot always control the initial influx of a thought, the Bible instructs us to *"take captive every thought to make it obedient to Christ"* (2 Corinthians 10:5). Meditation on scripture, prayer, gratitude, and surrender enables us to cooperate with the Holy Spirit's transformative work, allowing renewal that penetrates deep into our beliefs and subconscious mind.

This mental renewal is not mere self-discipline; it is spiritual formation. By intentionally renewing your mind, we create fertile soil for God to plant seeds of hope, faith, and divine vision. Over time the process of renewing your mind gets easier, suddenly the enemy might attempt to pop a lie into your head but your spirit replaces it with truth. For example you may hear a lie such as, "you failed", but suddenly you start saying, *"no that's a lie, I partner with God's truth, I haven't failed, I am an overcomer"*.

We put on a renewed mindset that aligns with God's promises—especially His promises about our deepest desires, such as motherhood. When our thoughts are transformed by God's truth, we become attuned to His perfect will and prepared to receive His blessings.

Luke 1:45 reveals the fruit of a renewed mind: true belief. Mary, despite tremendous uncertainty and societal challenges, embraced God's promise fully because her mind was aligned with heaven. She chose belief over doubt and expectancy over fear. Her faith exemplifies the kind of conviction that activates miracles.

For believers longing for a child, Mary's story encourages us to practice daily renewing of our minds. When we focus on God's promises, filling our thoughts with His truth, we cultivate a blessedness that opens the door to receive God's miraculous fulfilment. By replacing every lie with Scripture, we nurture faith that rises resilient even in the face of impossibility.

Abraham's story in Genesis is another inspiring example of faith in God's promise despite seemingly impossible circumstances. His wife Sarah, was ninety years old, long past childbearing years, God fulfilled His covenant by granting her a son, Isaac (Genesis 21:1-2). Abraham's faith was rooted in believing in God's power beyond human limitations.

Abraham's journey teaches us that God's timing and plans transcend our natural understanding. When believers cling to His promises with unwavering faith, even the impossible becomes possible. This story reminds us to be patient and steadfast, trusting God's perfect timing.

Hannah, the mother of the prophet Samuel, provides another biblical archetype of faith and perseverance. She endured years of barrenness, deeply lamenting and praying to God, yet did not give up believing. In 1 Samuel 1:27, she declares with faith, *"I prayed for this child, and the Lord has granted me what I asked of him."* Her story encourages believers to persist in prayer and faith, trusting that God hears and answers in His perfect time.

If you've been crying out to God in deep lament for a child, Hannah's testimony prophetically speaks into your life right now. Receive this breakthrough in your faith—a supernatural faith that transcends all understanding, as God moves powerfully to bless you with the baby your heart longs for.

Elizabeth's miraculous pregnancy with John the Baptist in her old age echoes Abraham's faithful waiting and Hannah's persistent prayers, proving God's timing transcends human limits. Barren and advanced in years, she and Zechariah received the angel Gabriel's promise: *their son would be great in the Lord's sight, filled with the Holy Spirit from the womb* (Luke 1:13-17).

When Mary visited, John leapt for joy in recognition of the Messiah, as Elizabeth declared under the Spirit's power, *"Blessed are you among women, and blessed is the fruit of your womb!"* (Luke 1:41-42). If you've clung to God's promises through barren seasons, Elizabeth's testimony speaks prophetically into your life right now—receive this supernatural breakthrough, as He opens your womb with the child your faith has prepared.

SCIENTIFIC EVIDENCE SUPPORTING FAITH AND MIND RENEWAL

Modern science recognises the profound link between emotional and mental well-being and physical health, particularly fertility. Research published in The Journal of Psychosomatic Obstetrics & Gynaecology (2020) shows that stress, anxiety, and unresolved emotional trauma negatively affect reproductive health and fertility rates. This corroborates the biblical instruction to cast our anxieties upon God and the spiritual necessity of renewing the mind.

Conversely, positive practices such as prayer, meditation, and affirmations—which align with biblical meditation and declaration—have been scientifically shown to reduce stress hormones like cortisol, improve hormone balance, and support reproductive function. These practices help foster an emotional environment conducive to conception and healthy pregnancy.

This integration of faith and science reveals that emotional healing complements spiritual readiness. As scripture teaches, the heart's condition influences the body, and renewal in the mind and spirit prepares us physically, emotionally, and spiritually for new life.

EMOTIONAL HEALING'S ROLE IN FERTILITY

The journey of hoping for a baby is often intertwined with emotional pain from past experiences—loss, trauma, or disappointment. Research in reproductive psychology reveals that unresolved emotional trauma can disrupt hormonal balance and ovulatory function. Healing emotional wounds through faith-based counselling, deliverance, or prayer ministry can restore inner peace, lower chronic stress, and create favourable conditions for conception.

This holistic healing aligns with Psalm 147:3: *"He heals the broken-hearted and binds up their wounds."* When the heart is healed, the body follows. Faith invites believers to seek healing not only in their physical bodies but deep in their spirits and emotions.

THE POWER OF DECLARATIONS AND AFFIRMATIONS

Declarations are more than positive speech—they are spiritual weapons that align our hearts and minds with God's Word. When we proclaim God's promises over our bodies, families, and wombs, we engage faith that activates heavenly power.

"Death and life are in the power of the tongue, and those who love it will eat its fruits" (Proverbs 18:21). Speaking faith-filled declarations nurtures belief by replacing doubt with hope, discouragement with joy.

Declarations for fertility faith include:

- "My body is a fertile ground for God's miracle."

- "I am fearfully and wonderfully made (Psalm 139:14), prepared for motherhood."

- "God's promises over my womb will not return void."

Each declaration invites the Holy Spirit to cultivate faith, trust, and expectancy in the believer's heart. Remember faith is a powerful force in action when we partner with God.

FAITH IN ACTION: PRACTICAL STEPS TO CULTIVATE BELIEF

Believing for a child requires intentional faith practices coupled with intentional renewal of the mind will bring supernatural transformation.

- **Daily Scripture Meditation:** Reflect on verses that affirm God's promises for families and children. Verses like Jeremiah 29:11 and Psalm 127:3 nurture hope.

- **Prayer and Fasting:** These spiritual disciplines invite God's power to breakthrough obstacles and open favour.

- **Community Support:** Surrounding oneself with prayer partners and faith community provides encouragement and accountability.

- **Journaling:** Write down struggles, prayers, and instances of answered faith to remind oneself of God's faithfulness.

- **Creative Expression:** Engage in worship, art, or music to express hope and invite God's presence.

These practical actions strengthen belief, build resilience against discouragement, and keep the heart expectant.

DECLARATIONS FOR FAITH AND MIND RENEWAL

- I declare that my mind is continually renewed by the Spirit of God, transforming my thoughts to align with His truth and promises.

- I choose to believe firmly and confidently, just as Hannah and Elizabeth did, trusting that God will fulfil every promise He has spoken over my life.

- By faith, I take every thought captive to obey Christ, releasing hope and expectancy that bring forth the blessings God has prepared for me.

- I reject lies of fear, doubt, and impossibility, and I embrace truth, joy, and faith in God's perfect plan.

- I declare emotional healing over my heart, peace over my spirit, and blessing over my womb.

REFLECTIONS FOR DAILY RENEWAL

- Which thoughts today reflect God's truth over my life's desires?

- Are there any recurring negative patterns or lies that I need to surrender and replace with Scripture?

- How have I seen God's faithfulness in small ways that encourage my belief in His promises?

- In what ways can I cultivate the same unwavering faith Mary, Sarah, Elizabeth and Hannah demonstrated?

SCRIPTURE MEDITATIONS

- Luke 1:45 — Blessed is she who believed.

- Romans 4:21 — Fully persuaded that God has power to do what He has promised.

- Romans 12:2 — Do not conform to the pattern of this world, but be transformed by the renewing of your mind.

- 2 Corinthians 10:5 — Take captive every thought to make it obedient to Christ.

- Hebrews 11:1 — Now faith is confidence in what we hope for and assurance about what we do not see.

- Psalm 147:3 — He heals the brokenhearted and binds up their wounds.

- 1 Samuel 1:27 — I prayed for this child, and the Lord has granted me what I asked of him.

She believed. Like Mary, Elizabeth, Sarah, and Hannah, believers longing for children are invited to root themselves deeply in God's promises through the renewing of their minds. By intentionally rejecting the lies of fear, doubt, and worldly thinking, and embracing faith, hope, and God's truth, we prepare not only our hearts but our whole beings to receive the abundant blessings God plans.

This chapter calls all believers to cultivate belief marked by conviction, perseverance, and hope—a belief that transforms possibility into reality and invites miracles into our lives and wombs.

Chapter 5

His Promises

"He did not waver at the promise of God through unbelief, but was strengthened in faith, giving glory to God, and being fully convinced that what He had promised He was able to perform" — Romans 4:20-22

The Bible is supernatural—filled with prophetic promises that have been, and continue to be, fulfilled in extraordinary ways. God's promises are as alive and relevant for us today as they were for those who first received them. He is not a man that He should lie, and His Word always accomplishes what He has spoken; it never returns void (Numbers 23:19; Isaiah 55:11).

The supernatural, according to the Bible, refers to everything that goes beyond the natural laws and abilities of this world—it is the spiritual realm where God's power, presence, and purposes override the limitations of what we see and understand. The supernatural is the unmistakable evidence of God's Kingdom breaking into our ordinary human experience.

Throughout Scripture, we witness miracles, healings, angelic encounters, divine provision, prophetic visions, and the outpouring of the Holy Spirit as clear demonstrations of the supernatural. From the opening words of Genesis—where God creates the world by speaking it into existence—to the resurrection of Jesus, the Bible makes it clear that God is not bound by natural limitations.

His supernatural works remind us that He is always able to do exceedingly and abundantly above all we ask or imagine (Ephesians 3:20).

Throughout the pages of Scripture, we discover countless testimonies of promises fulfilled in ways that defy natural explanation. The Bible is not just a historical record—it is a living testimony to God's miraculous power, love and faithfulness. When God speaks prophetically, those words carry supernatural authority and creative power—they are messages from His heart about our destiny and future.

Prophetic promises in the Bible are decrees from God that reveal His plans before they happen, inviting us to walk by faith and expect the impossible. They are declarations of what is to come, rooted in God's eternal truth and established by His Spirit. These promises are meant to spark hope, strengthen faith, and draw us closer to the One who makes the impossible possible.

As we reflect on these promises, we are reminded that God is still working today—He is able and willing to fulfil the prophetic words spoken over our lives, manifesting miracles in ways we cannot imagine. Our faith grows as we meditate on the supernatural nature of the Bible and embrace the power of prophetic promises and the exciting news is that we can prophetically declare the Bible into our own personal lives.

In Genesis 17, Abraham was ninety nine years old when God spoke to him about the promises of his son, Isaac. He believed without a shadow of a doubt that what God had promised, He would bring to pass. Faith reveals that faith is active, intentional, and resilient, even when circumstances suggest otherwise. Despite his advancing years and Sarah's barrenness, Abraham did not allow what was seen to dictate his belief. Instead, he anchored himself in the unseen promises of God.

Let us dwell deeply on what it means to be fully convinced in God's promises, as Abraham was fully convinced that God would come through with what He had promised him and Sarah and that was a baby. This unwavering conviction is the essence of deep faith. Being fully convinced in God's promises for us is a settled assurance, a spiritual certainty anchored in God's character and Word.

Why then do we struggle to believe in God's promises? Why do God's powerful promises sometimes seem distant or impossible? The answer is in what we are believing—is it a lie, or is it God's truth? The first lies appeared in the Garden of Eden, when God asked Adam and Eve, "Who told you that you were naked?" (Genesis 3:11). This pointed to the deceitful voice of the enemy that sowed doubt and shame in their hearts.

In seasons of longing—such as waiting for a child—those same voices echo: "Maybe God won't do it for me." These whispers may come from past disappointments, the world around us, or the enemy's deception. They plant seeds of unbelief that grow into barriers against faith. Recognising these lies is one of the first step toward freedom. As with Adam and Eve, God invites us to confront these voices and cling instead to His truth. Ask yourself: "Who told me that?" Was it God, or was it something or someone else?

When scripture says Abraham was *"fully convinced that God was able to do what He had promised"* (Romans 4:21), it highlights something critical: Abraham faced all discouraging facts but chose not to let them define his belief of the promises of God. He was surrounded by the same doubts and discouragements we face, yet he chose faith over fear, promise over probability.

This choice is foundational. Deep faith is not the absence of doubt but choosing God's voice over every other voice—even when doubt nags or logic contradicts hope. We all wrestle with that inner voice that says, "It won't happen for me" But those lies can lose their power when we take them captive to the obedience of christ or if we need to repent, then, as my spiritual Father would say, repent towards glistening hope, then renounce and surrender them to God and look to the promises and character of God

It is easy to allow the enemy's narrative—"you are too old," "your story is different," "maybe it won't happen"—to overshadow God's promises. These lies often sound logical or persistent because they feed on our fears, circumstances and experiences. But like Adam and Eve hiding after believing a lie, we often hide from the promises God has given us because of false shame or doubt.

To believe in God's promises, we must deliberately reject these lies. Deep faith is not the absence of doubts but choosing God's voice over every other. When disbelief rises, holding tightly to God's Word uproots the lies.

Personally, my journey with believing for my son Noah illustrates this deeply. There were seasons of waiting, some days uncertainty tried to creep in where the inner voice of doubt tried to speak louder than God's promises. Yet, time and again, I chose to fix my eyes on God's word and the promises He whispered to my heart.

Each scripture I meditated on, each declaration I spoke over Noah, fortified my faith. From the moment I received that promise of motherhood, I embraced it fully, rejecting the lies that whispered I was too old or that my story was unique and unlikely. Like Abraham, I believed by faith that God would fulfil his promise of blessing me with a child of my own and I was excited. When others might have labeled the situation as impossible, I stood fully convinced in the promises of God that He would come through for me.

Consider also Sarah from the Bible, who laughed when the promise of a child was first given because of her old age (Genesis 18:12). Yet that laughter transformed as she witnessed God's promise fulfilled in Isaac's birth. Similarly, Hannah's story from 1 Samuel 1 shows the power of deeply believing God's promise despite years of barrenness and societal pressure. Her persistent prayer and unwavering faith demonstrate the posture of being fully convinced despite the longest wait or the hardest trials.

The story of Hannah in 1 Samuel 1 offers additional encouragement. She waited many years for a child, deeply desired, and was mocked for her barrenness. But she did not give up. Through persistent prayer and surrender, God answered her longing with Samuel's birth. Hannah's example highlights that waiting in faith requires persistence and trust, even when there is silence or disappointment. Her story reminds us that God's timing is perfect, and enduring faith brings glory to God, just as Romans 4:20-22 affirms.

SCIENCE CONFIRMS THE POWER OF FAITH

Modern science increasingly confirms what Scripture has long taught: faith and hope have a powerful effect on our whole being—mind, body, and spirit. Neuroscience shows that hope and anticipation activate the brain's reward pathways, increase dopamine, and motivate perseverance, which beautifully echoes Hebrews 6:19: hope as an anchor for the soul.

Mindfulness practices combined with faith, such as meditative prayer and daily declarations, are shown to reduce anxiety and strengthen positive outlooks during difficult seasons. By repeatedly focusing on God's truth, we literally rewire our thoughts and build new neural pathways, which mental health research supports as crucial for lasting change.

Positive psychology further affirms the outcome-shaping power of belief and conviction. The "placebo effect" illustrates how deeply held beliefs can lead to real physiological changes, reinforcing the fact that being "fully convinced" is not only spiritual but also transforms our holistic health. Scientific research and Scripture together encourage us to move forward in faith—expectant that God's promises truly do shape our reality.

Recent studies in positive psychology and neuroscience show that when individuals practice hopeful anticipation and maintain a positive belief about their future, they experience increased motivation, emotional resilience, and even improved physical health.

This research validates the biblical call to hold fast to God's promises: as we expect good things—whether in prayer, declaration, or daily hope—our minds and bodies respond with greater strength and peace. Although science cannot measure spiritual miracles or guarantee specific outcomes, it confirms that the act of believing in promises, especially those rooted in faith, hope and meaning, generates tangible benefits that prepare us—spirit, soul, and body—to receive what we are believing for.

DECLARATIONS TO EMBRACE

- I declare that I am fully convinced God's promises are true and will come to pass in His perfect timing.

- I reject every lie that strengthens doubt or fear in my heart.

- My faith is rooted and grounded in God's unchanging Word, not circumstances around me.

- I embrace hope and trust in God's faithfulness, even during seasons of waiting.

- As Abraham believed against all odds, I believe that God's power is made perfect in my weakness.

REFLECTION QUESTIONS

- What lies about my situation do I need to recognise and reject today to strengthen my faith?

- How can I cultivate a daily habit of immersing myself in God's promises?

- In what ways has waiting shaped my character and understanding of God's faithfulness?

SCRIPTURES TO MEDITATE ON

- Romans 4:20-22 — Abraham's example of unwavering faith

- Hebrews 11:1 — "Now faith is confidence in what we hope for and assurance about what we do not see."

- Isaiah 40:31 — "But those who hope in the Lord will renew their strength..."

- Psalm 27:14 — "Wait for the Lord; be strong and take heart and wait for the Lord."

- Jeremiah 29:11 — "For I know the plans I have for you, declares the Lord, plans to prosper you not harm you, plans to give you hope and a future".

DECLARATIONS TO SPEAK OVER YOUR PROMISE

- I am fully convinced that God is able to do what He has promised me.

- No delay or doubt can overshadow the faithfulness of God in my life.

- I reject every lie that steals my hope and embrace the truth of God's Word.

- Like Abraham and Sarah, I believe that God's promises come to pass in His perfect timing.

- My faith is anchored in God's unchanging character, not my circumstances.

REFLECTIONS FOR YOUR JOURNEY

- Reflect on a promise from God that you find difficult to fully believe. What lies might be competing for your faith?

- How can you, like Abraham, anchor yourself daily in God's promises despite what you see?

- What spiritual disciplines (prayer, scripture meditation, declarations) can support your faith during waiting seasons?

FINAL ENCOURAGEMENT

The journey to believing in God's promises is ongoing. It requires daily returning to the Word and renewing the mind with God's promises and your heart's desires, declaring God's truth for your life, practicing faith, and consciously rejecting doubt. It is a posture of the heart that declares, "God is faithful; His promises are true." Like Abraham, let faith arise again and again, so that no matter the waiting, no matter the silence, your spirit & soul remains anchored in the certainty of God's faithful promises.

Faith is a powerful force and is the catalyst that transforms promises from words into realities. Be fully convinced to the prophetic promises of God and watch the miraculous unfold in your life.

Chapter 6
Speak Life

"There is life and death in the power of the tongue and those who speak it will eat its fruits"

Words are incredibly powerful. Scripture teaches us that there is life and death in the words we speak. When you think about your precious baby, your husband, your family, and your community, what thoughts and words do you carry deep within your heart? What beliefs have taken root so firmly that they inevitably come out through your speech?

Sometimes, we blurt out words we don't intend to. More often than not, these words come from hidden strongholds. Strongholds are long-held beliefs that have become part of the abundance of our hearts. These strongholds can be positive or negative. Negative strongholds represent lies or limiting beliefs the enemy has placed in our minds — thoughts that shape and control destructive words. Positive strongholds are truths from God that strengthen us, give us hope, and build our faith.

It's vital to remember: just as we can become trapped in negative mindsets, we can intentionally build strongholds based on God's word and His promises, infusing our hearts and minds with His truth.

When God says there is life and death in the power of the tongue, He is emphasising that what we say has the power to either build or destroy. Proverbs 21:23 warns, "Those who guard their mouths and their tongues keep themselves from calamity." So often, the words spoken over ourselves, our families, and our futures shape the environment we live in — emotionally, spiritually, and even physically.

Have you noticed how words of encouragement can lift your spirits, restore hope, and ignite faith? Conversely, harsh or negative words can wound, discourage, and even paralyse dreams. We bear a tremendous responsibility to steward our tongues carefully, knowing that those words will shape the reality we experience and the legacy we leave.

Jesus taught in Luke 6:45, "The mouth speaks what the heart is full of." In other words, what flows from our lips reflects what has taken residence in our hearts. If we desire to speak life, we must first examine what is abundant in our hearts. Are there lies, fears, and doubts hidden beneath the surface, waiting to be confessed? Or is God's truth and love the dominant narrative we carry?

Often, the words we speak — even unintentionally — expose these heart strongholds. Maybe you've said, "There's no hope for us to have a baby" or "It's too late for me." Such words reveal negative beliefs that must be brought into the light, repented of, and replaced with God's promises.

REPENT, RENOUNCE, AND REPLACE

In Chapter 1, I speak briefly on a powerful activation—to repent, renounce, and surrender the lies you have believed. In Chapter 11, I provide an in-depth activation for this practice. This is not a complicated process but a profound spiritual discipline. As soon as you identify a lie spoken or believed, confess it honestly to God, nail it to the cross, renounce it as false, and give it over to Jesus.

Then, replace it with biblical truth. For example, instead of "There is no hope," declare, "God is a God of hope, and He has plans to prosper me" (Jeremiah 29:11). This intentional replacement is what moves us from bondage into freedom.

The mind can be a battleground of warfare or a playground of childlike wonder and joy. The enemy desires to trap us in negative strongholds of fear, confusion, and despair, but by choosing to renew our minds with God's Word, we build positive strongholds rooted in His promises, light, and power.

I have heard many mothers say, *"I'm not telling anyone until three months, just in case."* Just in case what? That fear whispered a lie I refused to partner with. The moment I discovered I was pregnant, I told my nearest and dearest so they could cover Noah and I in prayer.

A dear sister in Christ shared the news that she was pregnant with a baby. She shared that her and her husband agreed that they would not tell anyone the news of their pregnancy until they were 12 weeks, she said, *"Just in case"*, I asked, *"Just in case what, Sis?"*, I began to share that this was a lie based on fear, she smiled and agreed, then shared the news with our church family the following week so we could all support her and her family in prayer. Today, she too is a proud mother of a beautiful boy.

PRACTICAL STEPS TO SPEAK LIFE

Speaking life is not just about positive thinking — it's an active spiritual practice. Here are some ways I use as a daily practice in my life, over time you will be able to identify lies instantly and replace them with truth until they become solid your mind:

- **Monitor your thoughts and words.** Be aware when negative or limiting words arise. Write them down if you must, then address them intentionally.

- **Confession and repentance.** When you catch yourself speaking or thinking lies, repent quickly. Invite the Holy Spirit to help you.

- **Speak Scripture aloud.** Verbalise God's promises in your life. For example: "I am fearfully and wonderfully made" (Psalm 139:14). "I am favoured and blessed".

- **Create declarations.** Develop personalised faith-filled affirmations you can say daily.

- **Surround yourself with life-giving input.** Listen to worship music, sermons, podcasts and testimonies that inspire hope.

- **Join a community.** Fellowship with people who speak life and faith over your journey.

When you become aware of a lie, do not slip into guilt or self-condemnation. Instead, thank God for bringing it into the light and celebrate His kindness by saying, "Thank You, Lord, for revealing this lie and showing me Your truth." God is not a God of condemnation; His heart is freedom and life. Scripture says you are set free and there is life in the Spirit. Romans 8:1–2 declares that *there is now no condemnation for those who are in Christ Jesus, for through Christ Jesus the law of the Spirit who gives life has set you free from the law of sin and death.*

ROLE OF FAITH IN SPEAKING LIFE

Faith is the key that gives life to our words and is a powerful force that can be used in both positive and negative language we use. Hebrews 11:1 defines faith as confidence in what we hope for and assurance about what we do not see. When our declarations rise from faith in God's character and promises, they carry creative power.

The battle is not our circumstances, the battle is in what we believe in our hearts. As you renew your mind and realign your heart with God's truth, your spoken words will naturally transform.

The entire Bible underscores the power of the tongue. James 3:5-12 offers both warning and hope, portraying the tongue as a small but mighty force capable of blessing or cursing. Jesus Himself used words to heal the sick, calm storms, and raise the dead (John 11:43). His teachings remind us that our words reveal the condition of our hearts and hold the power to consort with God's creative will or with enemy deception.

Our tongues do not only shape our individual lives but also influence families, communities and nations. Ephesians 4:29 exhorts us, *"Do not let any unwholesome talk come out of your mouths, but only what is helpful for building others up according to their needs."*

Through encouragement, prayers, and blessing over others, our words become instruments of healing and unity. Imagine the impact when churches, families, and friendships intentionally speak life rather than death!

SCIENCE AND THE POWER OF WORDS

Remarkably, science affirms the spiritual truth of speaking life. Studies on neuroplasticity show that our brain forms and strengthens neural pathways based on repeated thought patterns. Positive affirmations and confident speech literally reshape our brain to build resiliency and hope.

Dr. Carolyn Leaf, a respected cognitive neuroscientist, explains that forming new thought patterns requires repeated practice — three cycles of 21 days each to solidify new neural pathways. When you think a new thought repeatedly, your brain starts to hardwire those possibilities, replacing old, limiting pathways. Just 15 minutes of focused thought can begin this process.

This scientific understanding beautifully aligns with Romans 12:2, which speaks of transformation through the "renewing of your mind."

The word "re-" is a Latin prefix meaning "again" or "back," and it is used in English to form words that carry the idea of repetition, restoration, or returning to a previous state—for example, "renew" means to make new again. In the same way, renewing the mind is a discipline of intentionally reprogramming our thoughts with God's truth again and again, in partnership with faith.

Mindfulness and meditation research also reveals that combining focused positive thought with prayer reduces stress hormones and produces emotional regulation. Thus, spiritual disciplines of speaking life align with the latest health science about human wellbeing.

WALKING IN AUTHORITY AS GOD'S CHILD

Because Jesus defeated death and sin on the cross, we now speak with authority over lies and destructive forces. Mark 11:23 declares, "If anyone says to this mountain, 'Go, throw yourself into the sea,' and does not doubt, but believes... it will be done."

Our words, when spoken in faith, carry authority to move mountains and open doors previously shut. This authority demands responsibility: we must choose to declare God's truth consistently.

Understanding the power of our words transforms us from passive receivers to empowered co-creators with God. When we speak life, we actively participate in God's unfolding plan for our lives and those around us. This is the doorway to deeper faith, expectation, and joy. No longer resigned to circumstances, we become faith warriors sowing hope and life with every word.

During my preparation season for Noah, I discovered that faith-filled declarations were lifesaving. As doubts nipped at my heels, daily speaking of scriptures like Jeremiah 29:11, Psalm 139 and Hebrews 11:1 became my spiritual armour.

I confessed daily that I was in a preparation season for a baby and I thanked God every time doubt tried to creep. These words, spoken with faith, rewired my inner dialogue and strengthened hope amid uncertainty.

You too can find words and promises to declare over your journey, tailoring them to your circumstances and deepening your walk with God.

DAILY HABITS TO PRACTICE SPEAKING LIFE

Develop these spiritual habits to cultivate life-giving speech:

- Start and end each day by speaking God's promises aloud.

- Write a journal recording how God's words bring transformation.

- Incorporate prayer walks with spoken affirmations.

- Celebrate answered prayers to build faith reminders.

- Form or join a community committed to speaking life and encouragement.

REFLECTION QUESTIONS FOR YOUR JOURNEY

- What negative words or thoughts have I spoken that I need to confess and renounce?

- What promises will I declare daily to build positive strongholds?

- How will I intentionally speak life into others' lives consistently?

SCRIPTURES TO MEDITATE ON

- Proverbs 18:21 — The power of the tongue

- Luke 6:45 — The heart's abundance shown in speech

- Romans 12:2 — Renewing the mind

- 2 Corinthians 10:5 — Taking thoughts captive

- James 3:5-10 — The tongue's impact

- Ephesians 4:29 — Speaking to build up others

- Mark 11:23 — Speaking to move mountains

- Psalm 139:14 — Fearfully and wonderfully made

- Jeremiah 29:11 — God's plans for hope

CLOSING WORDS OF ENCOURAGEMENT

Speak life intentionally. Your words are seeds planted in the fertile soil of your heart and the hearts of those around you. What you sow will grow and bear fruit in your life and community.

By choosing to repent of lies, renew your mind with God's truth, and declare His promises with faith, you lay the foundation for miracles, healing, and abundant life.

Let every word you speak become an act of faith — a powerful seed of life that blossoms into God's glory in your story and beyond.

Chapter 7

Faith-Filled Speech for Motherhood

"If we bridle our tongue, we can bridle our whole body."

I used to be someone who, after praying fervently for a baby, would immediately fall into worry about the very thing I had just prayed for. I would ruminate on the 'what ifs' and doubts, unintentionally speaking curses over my own prayers because I had failed to attach faith to what I had declared. This personal revelation taught me the crucial importance of controlling what words I speak after praying—especially concerning something as precious and longed for as a child.

Your journey to motherhood is deeply influenced by the words you speak, because what you declare in faith begins to shape the reality you will walk out as a mother. The power of your words—faith-filled, confident, hopeful—can lift your spirit, renew your hope, and open the door for God's blessings to come to life. Conversely, words spoken in worry or doubt can create strongholds that hold you captive in fear.

What words are you speaking after your prayers for a baby?

Are you finding worry creeping in? Are you speaking fear about the circumstances, the timing, or physical limitations? Are you allowing your past circumstances dictate to your future? If so, know this: the Bible calls this out gently but firmly. Bridling your tongue—controlling what you say—is not just good advice but a spiritual necessity.

James 3:2-3 tells us, "If we put bits into the mouths of horses to make them obey us, we can turn the whole animal." This vivid illustration reminds us that our tongue, though small, is a powerful instrument. It can steer the entire course of our lives, just as a small bit controls a mighty horse. To bridle our tongue means to tame it—to intentionally control what we say, when we say it, and the attitude with which we say it. It means choosing words that build up rather than tear down, words that declare God's promises instead of doubt or fear.

When we speak words of faith and blessing over the process of having a baby—declaring life, hope, and promise—we are aligning our hearts and spirit with God's good and perfect plan. Conversely, if after prayer we allow words of negativity, worry, or doubt to take root, this can limit the spiritual authority granted to us through prayer. As the Apostle James warns, "The tongue is a fire, a world of evil among the parts of the body. It corrupts the whole person, sets the whole course of their life on fire…" (James 3:5-6).

In the context of praying for a baby, the discipline of bridling our tongue looks like this:

- Rejecting fear and worry after prayer, trusting that God's promises are sure and will come to pass.

- Speaking life and blessing into every thought, conversation, and circumstance related to conception and birth.

- Guarding the heart, as the heart is the wellspring of life and words.

- Recognising that what we say reflects and influences our emotions, actions, and spiritual walk.

The tongue is connected deeply to the heart. Therefore, guarding our speech is also guarding our faith and hope. When our words align with faith, prayer becomes powerful and effective. When worry and negative speech dominate, they can sabotage even the most fervent prayers.

I want to share a personal part of my story to encourage you. When I was waiting and praying for my son, Noah, I struggled with this very challenge. I would passionately pray and then immediately worry—wondering if His promise were really for me. I realised that my words following prayer weren't always words of faith. Sometimes they echoed fear or doubt, unintentionally mixing God's promises with my own insecurities.

But God gently showed me that what I say after prayer needs to be filled with faith-filled declarations and hope, not anxiety. I began daily speaking scriptures aloud over myself and my womb, speaking life into my situation. I attached faith to my prayers and began thanking the Lord for what He has already done. It was a healing process—not instant, but transformational—as I reined in my tongue, surrendered fear, and declared God's truth instead.

This change didn't just affect my emotions or beliefs; it transformed my very spirit. Faith-filled speech coupled with the excitement of God's promise of a baby became an act of worship and alignment with God's desire to bless me with motherhood.

So this leads me to this, what are we believing for ourselves, does our beliefs line up to God's truths or does it line up with lies? This is really important in life, in order to walk out in freedom, we must be first ask God what lies am I believing? I know I have talked about this before in previous chapters but this is really important because the enemy wants us to believe in contrary to God's word, His promises, prophetic words and His truth for us.

For many years I allowed the enemies lies to steer my life. Circumstances and events that lead me to believe these lies affected how I saw myself for many years until God gently reminded me of the truth of my identity in Him and His perfect promises for my life.

If we want to overcome negative circumstances in our lives then we must first invite Holy Spirit in revealing the belief that is the lie in that area and asking God who He says we are. This is such a powerful and transformative process that can unlock freedom in every area of our lives especially where we desire to start a family and have children.

The words you choose to speak daily have profound effects on your body, mind, and soul. Stressful thoughts and pessimistic language increase cortisol, the stress hormone, impacting fertility and overall health. Positive affirmations and hopeful declarations not only nurture your mental health but create physiological environments conducive to miracles, including conception.

Faith-filled speech releases peace, reduces anxiety, and strengthens resilience—the very conditions needed as you wait in God's timing.

Science confirms the power of words, belief, and mindset in influencing outcomes. Neuroscience tells us that the brain rewires itself through neuroplasticity; habits and beliefs are formed or dismantled by the repetition of thoughts and speech.

Cognitive neuroscientist Dr. Carolyn Leaf explains that switching toxic thought patterns to positive ones requires repeating new thoughts for about three 21-day cycles three cycles of this will solidify it, allowing the brain to build new neural pathways (Leaf, 2018).

This scientific principle fits beautifully with scripture's call to "renew our minds" (Romans 12:2). Repetition of God's truth—aided by declarations and meditations in His Word—rewires not just our minds but our spirits, making faith a tangible, living force.

SCRIPTURE TO ANCHOR YOUR FAITH

Your story is written in Heaven with great love and care. God promises:

"For I know the plans I have for you," declares the Lord, "plans to prosper you and not to harm you, plans to give you hope and a future" (Jeremiah 29:11).

Your calling to motherhood is part of that plan.

Psalm 139:16 assures you of God's intimate involvement in your life: "Your eyes saw my unformed body; all the days ordained for me were written in your book before one of them came to be."

Deuteronomy 7:9 reminds us of God's faithfulness across generations: "Know therefore that the Lord your God is God; he is the faithful God, keeping his covenant of love to a thousand generations…"

You carry a beautiful legacy in your womb, one that God is preparing for something wonderful—a generational blessing.

WHAT WORDS WILL YOU SPEAK TODAY?

Here are some faith-filled examples for you to declare daily:

- "I am so excited—God is blessing us with a baby!" (Celebrate by preparing baby clothes or other joyful activities, this is an act of faith in God, hope for the future and love for the desires of your heart).

- "Thank You, Lord, for the beautiful child You are creating within me."

- "God's timing is perfect, and I trust His plans for my motherhood journey."

- "I am a mother, called and blessed by God."

- "Every cell in my body is aligning to bring new life."

Paired with these declarations, take moments to visualise your pregnancy—the joy of holding your baby, the peace of walking in God's promises. Visualisation, combined with faith-filled speech, further awakens hope and rewires the brain and enlightens your spirit to see your blessing.

YOUR TONGUE IS A GATEWAY TO YOUR DESTINY

Your speech is a spiritual gatekeeper, opening or closing doors to your destiny. Jesus said, *"Out of the overflow of the heart the mouth speaks"* (Matthew 12:34). What you say not only reflects your current state but also influences your future reality.

When you speak fear or doubt, you close the door to the full manifestation of God's blessing. When you speak faith, hope, and life, you open the door wide for God's promises to walk in.

I want to remind you: your words have creative power because the Spirit of God lives within you. You are His beloved daughter, entrusted with authority to declare His blessings over your body, womb, and motherhood.

THE BATTLE IS REAL, BUT VICTORY IS ASSURED

Spiritual warfare is real. The enemy will try to bring discouragement, whispers of "It's too late," or "You are no longer able." But remember, in God, you are more than a conqueror (Romans 8:37). The victory belongs to you when you refuse to let lies find a home in your tongue or heart.

Each day you declare life, you build spiritual momentum that weakens these lies. The more you speak God's Word, the stronger your faith becomes, the louder your voice of hope sings, and your soul grows resilient.

PRAYER AND FAITH-FILLED SPEECH GO HAND IN HAND

Prayer is powerful, but it is only as effective as the faith that backs it up. If your heart wavers or your words follow prayer with worry, you can inadvertently limit God's ability to work.

As you pray, speak as if the promise is already coming to pass. Father, thank You for the child You are bringing forth. I praise You for Your perfect timing and faithfulness. Let my words be pleasing to You, grounded in unwavering faith.

CELEBRATE EVERY STEP—NO MATTER HOW SMALL

I encourage you to celebrate progress on the journey—no matter how small. Each indication that God is answering your prayers, whether it's a hopeful medical report, a peaceful night's sleep, or an encouraging word from a friend, is worth proclaiming.

Celebrate by speaking joy-filled words. "Thank You, Lord, for this breakthrough." "I am grateful for every moment of peace You give me." These declarations keep your heart hopeful and align your spirit with God's goodness.

PRACTICAL TIPS FOR DAILY FAITH-FILLED SPEECH

- **Begin your day with scripture aloud.** Read and declare verses that encourage you as a mother.

- **Write a faith journal.** Record prayers, declarations, and signs of hope or answered prayer.

- **Surround yourself with encouraging voices.** Join Bible study groups, listen to worship music, or podcasts that build your faith.

- **Visualise your journey.** Spend moments imagining holding your baby, hearing the first laugh, naming your child, trusting God's promises deeply.

- **Repeat key declarations.** "I am a vessel of God's blessing," "God's promises are alive in me," "I trust His plan for my motherhood."

YOUR WORDS CAN CHANGE YOUR STORY

Your words are seeds planting your destiny. You might be in the most challenging season of waiting, I encourage you to change your perspective, flip the story and see this 'wilderness season' as a 'preparation season' your faith-filled speech waters the seeds of your miracle. Each kind, hopeful, and God-centered word invites God's power to move in your womb and your life.

Remember, God's Word never returns void (Isaiah 55:11). Your commitment to speak life over your motherhood journey is a declaration that you trust God's promise beyond what you see.

DECLARATIONS FOR YOUR HEART AND LIFE

- I bridle my tongue and speak words of faith, hope, and life.

- I declare God's promises over my womb and future family.

- Every wonder-working word I speak plants seeds of blessing and miracle.

- My heart is fixed on God's faithfulness, and my words reflect His truth.

- I am a blessed and expecting mother, filled with joy and confident hope.

REFLECTIONS TO MEDITATE ON

- What words are you speaking after your prayers? Are they life-giving or limiting?

- How can you develop the discipline to bridle your tongue and guard your speech each day?

- What is one scripture you can declare aloud daily to strengthen your heart?

SCRIPTURES FOR MEDITATION

- James 3:2-12 (On the tongue's power)

- Proverbs 18:21 (Life and death in the power of the tongue)

- Jeremiah 29:11 (God's plan to prosper you)

- Psalm 139:13-16 (God's intricate design)

- Romans 8:37 (More than conquerors)

- Isaiah 40:31 (Renewed strength in waiting)

FINAL WORDS OF ENCOURAGEMENT

God's mighty power is alive within you. Your words are gifts, tools of faith that can uphold the promise of motherhood. Choose each day to bridle your tongue, overpower worry with hope, and speak

God's promises boldly. As you do, you position yourself for the miraculous, aligning your spirit with heaven's truth.

Give yourself some grace, within the pages of this book are words of encouragement, choose one scripture, one meditation that speaks to you in this season and lean into them with the Lord and meditate on it. Psalm 1:2 declares, *"But his delight is in the law of the LORD, and on his law he meditates day and night."*

I am excited for you—God is moving. Your faith-filled speech is the soundtrack of your miracle in action. Keep speaking, keep believing, keep walking in hope. Your baby is worth every word of faith you declare.

Chapter 8:

Spirit and Life

"The words I speak to you are spirit, and they are life."
— Jesus (John 6:63)

In previous chapters, we discussed the power of words and how our words have the ability to influence our circumstances. Jesus tells us in John 6:63, *"the words I speak to you—they are spirit, and they are life"*. Today, I want to focus on what it means for our words to carry spirit.

What does it mean for our words to have spirit upon them? In Matthew 6:10, Jesus teaches His disciples how to pray, saying, *"Thy kingdom come, Thy will be done on earth as it is in heaven"* (Matthew 6:10). Here, Jesus reveals that the words we speak are not merely human expressions; they release spirit into the atmosphere. This spirit is powerful because it connects us to the Kingdom of God, which is accessed and experienced through the Spirit.

In other words, when we speak in alignment with God's will, our words carry the very life and power of His Spirit, helping to bring heavenly realities into the earthly realm. This teaches us that our speech is a spiritual force, able to affect both the unseen spiritual atmosphere and the tangible circumstances around us. Through this understanding, we recognise the importance of speaking words filled with faith, life, and God's kingdom authority.

Jesus's words in John 6:63, is not just beautiful poetry—it's a spiritual principle that every longing mother can cling to. Our words, when aligned with God's Word, don't just float into space; they become active, powerful, Spirit-filled life.

Our stories often begin with our thoughts and words—even before our prayers ever take shape. As a woman longing for a baby, you may find yourself whispering hopes in the night, wondering if anyone hears. Yet, right from the start, God teaches that words matter: His own creative power was released through words. *"And God said, 'Let there be light'—and there was light"* (Genesis 1:3).

Jesus said, *"Greater things you will do because I go to my Father"* (John 14:12). This means that Jesus has given us power and authority to do what He does and even greater things. What would that look like if Jesus says His words are spirit and life and we walk in the same power and authority He does, then our words are spirit and life.

I find it so fascinating and exciting because we are spirit beings having a human experience. I know this can sound new age but it's not; throughout scripture, Jesus calls us to connect with our spirit. He speaks of spiritual eyes, ears, and mouth, which could only mean we are also spiritual beings with spiritual senses. For example, Jesus said, "Blessed are your eyes, for they see, and your ears, for they hear" (Matthew 13:16), highlighting a spiritual perception that goes beyond natural sight and sound. Similarly, Paul reminds us that "the eyes of your heart may be enlightened" (Ephesians 1:18), emphasising the power of spiritual imagination and vision to perceive God's truth and promises.

This spiritual seeing allows us to envision God's Kingdom realities even before they manifest physically. It's like faith's eyes that gaze beyond current circumstances into the realm where God's word is active and powerful (Hebrews 11:1). When we speak with the spirit-filled life Jesus describes, our words become vessels of life, healing, and transformation, releasing the Kingdom into our atmosphere. Proverbs 18:21 underscores this truth: *"Death and life are in the power of the tongue"* (Proverbs 18:21), revealing the authority our spoken words carry.

Therefore, Jesus entrusting us with the power and authority of words rich with spirit and truth (John 6:63) invites us not only to speak but to see and hear spiritually—to align all our senses to the spiritual realm through Jesus Christ with Holy Spirit guidance. Just as Ezekiel was trusted to speak life over dry bones (Ezekiel 37), so are we called to use our spiritual senses to declare life over our dreams and circumstances.

My spiritual mother, Wendy Backlund, teaches that faith is the seed of our imagination—an active, living force that plants God-given visions in our spiritual mind. It is like having eyes of faith that look beyond current circumstances into the unseen realm where God's Word is active and powerful (Hebrews 11:1). In this way, her teaching shows faith as a creative seed that awakens and fuels our spiritual imagination.

She says that faith allows us to envision unseen possibilities, planting them as seeds in the fertile soil of our imagination. This spiritual sight transcends the limits of current reality, empowering us to mentally and spiritually see the fulfilment of God's promises before they manifest physically.

Faith as a seed in the imagination aligns with Hebrews 11:1's description of faith as *"being sure of what we hope for and certain of what we do not see,"* because it involves purposefully imagining the reality of God's word taking root and growing into fruitfulness in our lives.

Therefore, faith is not passive or wishful thinking—it is an intentional spiritual act, sowing seeds of imagination that God's word energises and brings to life. This vision through faith's eyes creates momentum toward breakthrough, serving as the foundation for declarations and actions grounded in God's truth.

This teaching encourages us to cultivate our faith by nurturing the imagination with God's promises, knowing that what we imagine in faith is the seed of what God will harvest in our lives.

God created our imaginations, I believe He is calling us up higher to activate our spiritual senses and see, hear and speak what He sees, hears and speaks. It is an exciting time for us. Visualising what we want to see for our lives is such a powerful and transformative way to *"call those things as that are not as though they are"* Romans 4:17.

Recently the Lord gave me a revelation from Psalm 100:4 which says, *"Enter into His gates with thanksgiving and His courts with praise; give thanks to him and praise His name,"* Close your eyes and Imagine stepping into the spiritual realm and entering through a gate into

His courts in Heaven, not just as a physical act, but as a spiritual breakthrough,—where gratitude and praise become the key to unlocking deeper levels to freedom in your life that brings you closer to God.

Thanksgiving isn't just polite or routine; it's a divine password, an invitation that ushers you into the very presence and spirit of God, allowing you to celebrate instead of striving for perfection. This act of gratitude and praise releases you from stagnation, and propels you into higher spiritual dimension where your spirit becomes one with Gods spirit, and answered prayers and breakthroughs begin to unfold like never before.

As you enter through His gates with thanksgiving and His courts with praise, you are stepping into transformational breakthrough in key areas of your life like never before. Right now God is inviting you into new levels of breakthrough in the areas you have been praying for, calling you into a fuller, richer experience of His grace and goodness.

On the other side of the gate, you will find yourself advancing into higher spiritual dimensions of your faith walk—new depths in your relationship with others & God, fresh wisdom and revelation, greater freedom, and overflowing joy & peace. This is not just an entrance; it's a powerful passage into spiritual, transformational breakthrough, fuelled by a heart of thanksgiving and praise to the one who fearfully and wonderfully made you.

YOUR PREPARATION SEASON: LEARNING THE LANGUAGE OF SPIRIT AND LIFE

When I entered my own preparation season, I realised God was inviting me to steward my internal dialogue as much as my external steps. I began to observe the words I spoke—especially on hard days. Were they filled with doubt, or grounded in the hope that God's Word, which is spirit and life, is stronger than my circumstance?

One verse that ministered to me during this season was Joshua 1:8: *"This book of the law shall not depart from your mouth, but you shall meditate on it day and night, that you may observe to do according to all that is written in it. For then you will make your way prosperous, and then you will have good success."* (Joshua 1:8)

It's no coincidence that before Joshua entered the Promised Land, God didn't just say, "be brave"—He told him to speak, meditate, and declare God's Word continually. The promised life was on the other side of aligning his tongue and mind with truth—truth rooted in spirit and life.

As women on this sacred path, we do the same. We speak words brimming with promise—words infused with the spirit and life of Jesus—even when our hearts ache. We nurture not only our physical health but our hope through spirit-led vocabulary that releases the spirit and life of God into our circumstances.

WORDS AS SEEDS: SCRIPTURAL FOUNDATIONS IN SPIRIT AND LIFE

Proverbs 18:21 declares, *"Death and life are in the power of the tongue, and those who love it will eat its fruit".* This profound truth shows that our words are seeds—spirit-filled seeds—that bear fruit according to what we plant. When you are aspiring to mother a child, every confession, declaration, and whispered hope—even when seemingly small—matters because they carry the Spirit and Life Jesus spoke of.

Paul gently exhorts us, *"Let no corrupt word proceed out of your mouth, but what is good for necessary edification, that it may impart grace to the hearers"* (Ephesians 4:29). Your words not only build you up but also those around you—your spouse, your promised child, your family, church family and community. When your words are filled with spirit and life, they become channels of grace and healing.

Even when the journey feels lonely or uncertain, keep speaking life and hope through scriptures such as:

- "My God will supply all my needs" (Philippians 4:19)

- "The Lord will bless me with a future filled with hope" (Jeremiah 29:11)

- "I will not miscarry or be barren; the Lord will give me a full lifespan" (Exodus 23:26)

Remember, these declarations are not just hopeful phrases—they are Spirit-breathed words through which God's power flows, shaping your reality and activating His promises.

SCIENTIFIC EVIDENCE: THE POWER OF THOUGHT AND WORD

Modern neuroscience confirms what the Bible has proclaimed for centuries: Our thoughts and words shape the world inside—and even outside—of us. It starts within.

Dr. Caroline Leaf, a Christian neuroscientist, has pioneered research on how our thought life changes our brains, emotions, and bodies. In her book *Switch On Your Brain*, she explains, "75 to 98 percent of mental, physical, and behavioural illness comes from one's thought life." Dr. Leaf's research reveals that our minds are neuroplastic—meaning we can literally rewire our brains by choosing to dwell on life-giving thoughts and words.

Dr. Leaf states:
"You are not a victim of your biology. Your mind is powerful, and you are able to renew your mind daily."

She teaches a five-step "neurocycle" rooted in both scripture and science: recognise toxic thought patterns, reflect, write out your declarations, take action, and practice faith-filled thinking. This process is deeply biblical, echoing Paul's instruction to *"take every thought captive to Christ"* (2 Corinthians 10:5) and to *"renew your mind"* (Romans 12:2).

Research from other Christian neuroscientists, such as Dr. Daniel Amen and Dr. Curt Thompson, also affirms that words of hope, gratitude, and faith can decrease stress hormones and activate parts of the brain related to healing and optimism. Positive declarations—powered by scripture—can literally prepare your body for new life, reduce anxiety, and promote hormonal balance essential for fertility.

SPIRIT AND LIFE: FINAL ENCOURAGEMENT

When Jesus said, "The words I speak to you are spirit and life" (John 6:63), He revealed the secret to shifting the very atmosphere around us. Our declarations align us with the Holy Spirit, who moves to create, heal, and bring order out of chaos.

You have the God-given ability to speak life over your womb, your dreams, and your preparation season. Every courageous faith-filled word is like water to dry ground, a morning sun on the seeds of faith sown in your heart.

Let the words you speak be filled with the Spirit—words that release hope, not fear; wholeness, not brokenness; and life, not despair.

SCRIPTURE STUDY—A DAILY FEAST

Make scripture your daily nourishment. Beyond the verses already mentioned, consider these additional passages as spiritual food, each one handpicked for mothers in their preparation season:

- **Isaiah 43:19** – "See, I am doing a new thing! Now it springs up; do you not perceive it?"
  This verse reminds you that God is always at work, even in hidden ways. New things spring forth where you least expect—hold hope for miracles not yet seen.

- **Romans 8:28** – "We know that in all things God works for the good of those who love Him, who have been called according to His purpose."

God weaves every detail together for your good, even when the threads seem tangled. Trust His higher wisdom.

- **Psalm 34:4-5** – "I sought the LORD, and he answered me; he delivered me from all my fears. Those who look to him are radiant; their faces are never covered with shame."
  Let God's presence and promises be your shield against anxiety and discouragement. He exchanges shame for shining radiance.

- **Proverbs 4:23** – "Above all else, guard your heart, for everything you do flows from it."
  Guard your heart with hopeful, faithful thoughts. Speak gratitude and forgiveness to yourself, and keep bitterness far away.

CIRCLE OF BLESSING— COMMUNITY AND INTERCESSION

No woman should navigate her preparation season alone. God designed us for community, comfort, and shared wisdom. Build a "Circle of Blessing"—find two or three trusted women or couples who can join you in prayer, encouragement, and love. Share your journey, victories, and honest struggles.

James 5:16 teaches, *"Therefore confess your sins to each other and pray for each other so that you may be healed. The prayer of a righteous person is powerful and effective."* Inviting prayer, testimony, and support brings healing and releases God's favour.

Celebrate together each milestone—a doctor's appointment, a heartfelt breakthrough, or just a peaceful day. Shared joy magnifies hope.

GENTLE VISUALISATION & REFLECTION EXERCISE

At the close of each day, spend a few moments in stillness, visualise life inside your womb, use your senses and attach faith.

Then spend some time reflecting on these questions, ask yourself:

- What promises from God brought light to my heart today?

- Where did I feel afraid or discouraged, and how did God meet me?

- What words did I speak that reflected faith and hope? Where could I gently improve tomorrow?

- Is there a fear I need to release, or gratitude I need to express before sleep?

End with a soft prayer: "Lord, thank you for being my Spirit and Life. I trust your goodness and surrender my desires into your loving hands."

DECLARATION OF BLESSING—
A WHISPER FOR EVERY DAUGHTER

- "I am preparing for life with sacred joy; God is nearer than my breath."

- "My womb, mind, and heart are aligned with hope and faith."

- "Love leads me each day; I rise in courage and trust."

- "Every cell in my body, every thought in my mind is renewed by the Spirit and Word of God."

- "My future is filled with blessing, testimony, and radiant grace."

FINAL SCRIPTURAL MEDITATION

Sit quietly with these words:

- Isaiah 43:19 – "See, I am doing a new thing!"

- Psalm 139 – "You knit me together in my mother's womb."

- Joshua 1:9 – "Be strong and courageous...the Lord your God is with you wherever you go."

- 1 Corinthians 13 – "Faith, hope, and love remain."

- Romans 8:28 – "In all things God works for the good..."

Breathe them in as daily bread, letting God's Spirit and life flow through every part of your preparation season.

Let your journey be saturated with kindness, patience, and gentle expectation. Trust that your words, prayers, thoughts, and spiritual disciplines truly shape your destiny, all under the loving gaze of your Heavenly Father. Your story is one of life, hope, and the beauty of Spirit-filled motherhood.

Chapter 9

Gives Life

*"God who gives life to the dead and calls those things that do not
exist as though they did."* — Romans 4:17

One of the most beautiful revelations in the journey of faith is that
God is the giver of life—even where things seem barren, broken,
or impossible. This truth is at the core of our preparation season
as mothers-in-waiting.

Romans 4:17 speaks directly to the heart of every woman longing
for a child: *"God…gives life to the dead and calls into being things that
were not."* These words have carried me through discouragement,
weaving hope into empty places, and inviting me to believe that
what seems impossible is within God's loving reach.

Romans 4:17 speaks into God breathing life into those places of
our lives where we feel stagnant or stuck, He instructs us to declare
for those things that are the desires of our hearts and if your desire
is start a family then the Lord is saying to you today to breath life

over you and your husband and believe for the baby that the Lord has promised you.

God showed Ezekiel a valley full of dry bones, a picture of utter lifelessness. He told Ezekiel to prophesy—to speak His word over those dead places—until life arose (Ezekiel 37:1-14). God could have simply restored the bones Himself, but He gives Ezekiel power and authority to speak into the bones to speak life into the bones by giving Him a voice.

This story is more than history—it's a living principle for us today. In our seasons of waiting, especially when longing for a baby, we may feel like our dreams resemble dry bones. But God invites us into partnership: *"Prophesy to these bones and say, 'Dry bones, hear the word of the Lord!"* (Ezekiel 37:4).

Our words, spoken with faith, infused with hope become vehicles for resurrection. We are called to speak life in our circumstances, to prophesy over ourselves, our husbands, our family, our hopes, our wombs, and even to places of disappointment or pain.

In my season of preparation, I learned that prophecy begins at home—in my heart, in my thoughts, and in my spoken words. When the Lord gave me the revelation that I was in a preparation season for Noah, I got excited, I praised the Lord in every circumstance, no matter what, I was going to prophecy life over my baby, declare it and believe that God was giving me the desires of my heart.

I realised my preparation season was more than waiting; it was an active, faith-filled journey in God's covenant and creative power. God gives us the power and authority to declare life over the dry areas of our lives. It is so exciting that we can partner with Him,

His promises and His truth and I love that God invites us to partner with his creative power because when we do, we get to see the
dry bones in our lives come alive.

THE POWER AND AUTHORITY WE ARE GIVEN

God's choice to have Ezekiel speak, instead of acting alone,
demonstrates the trust and authority He gives us. We are invited
to co-labor with Heaven—to speak forth what God has already
willed, calling things that seem non-existent into reality.

This invitation is evident in Jesus' words: *"Truly I tell you, if anyone
says to this mountain, 'Go, throw yourself into the sea,' and does not doubt
in their heart but believes… it will be done for them"* (Mark 11:23). Here,
mountains represent obstacles—sometimes even the invisible
barriers to becoming a mother. God gives us authority to speak,
believe, and act in faith, trusting Him for the outcome.

You may have internalised lies along your path: "This isn't my
portion," "I am too old," "Something is wrong with me." As you
read these words, know that God's truth is higher, feelings of hopelessness, while they seem real, do not validate God's truth, they
only validate what you believe to be true in that moment.

God's word and promises are truth. He has given you power and
authority to prophesy life over your situation and invite His Spirit
to breathe into your waiting.

SCIENTIFIC EVIDENCE: THE BRAIN'S POWER TO RESTORE AND GIVE LIFE

Dr. Caroline Leaf, teaches extensively about the way our thoughts and words literally reshape our brain and body. She writes, "As you think, you change the structure of your brain." (Leaf, 2013).

When we rehearse and speak God's truth—filling our minds and mouths with life-filled declarations—our brains form powerful new pathways. These positively-formed neural networks can help regulate immune function, balance hormones, and improve emotional well-being. Dr. Leaf's studies show that intentional focus on life-giving words is not simply "optimism"—it is a scientific, God-designed mechanism to prepare our bodies for the miracle of conception and healing.

Think about this: every time you declare God's promise, your brain and body cooperate with the Spirit to welcome new life.

PROPHESYING LIFE INTO YOUR PREPARATION SEASON

What does it look like to prophesy life as a woman preparing for a baby? Begin by speaking God's promises in the face of apparent obstacles:

- "I declare my womb is healthy and receptive to life."
- "I call forth God's blessings on my body, my family, and my promised child."
- "Where there was once emptiness, there is now fullness of joy."

- "I renounce every curse spoken over my fertility and claim God's covenant blessing."

Your words, spoken in faith, infused with hope and in line with scripture, act as seeds sown into fertile spiritual soil. The power God has given you will bear fruit as you persist, watering those seeds with gratitude and trust.

THE BLESSINGS OF GENERATIONS

God is a God of legacy. Romans 4:17 says He *"gives life"*—not just for one moment, but for generations. In Genesis 17:7, He promises, *"I will establish my covenant between Myself, you and your descendants after you for the generations to come."* This is an eternal promise: God delights in blessing children, families, and future lineages. Your preparation for motherhood is not only for you—it is for generations yet to be born.

Exodus 23:26 reassures: *"None will miscarry or be barren in your land. I will give you a full life span."* These words are for every woman who has feared an empty future; God's promise is abundance, joy, and life multiplied.

Many women on the journey to motherhood know the sting of disappointment. Perhaps there have been negative reports, unsuccessful cycles, or seasons where hope felt out of reach. If this is your story, remember that God specialises in rewriting narratives. The valley of dry bones in Ezekiel's vision was not a place of defeat—it was the birthplace of a revival.

Dr. Caroline Leaf teaches that negative thinking patterns can polarise us into unhealthy cycles, but, through intentional daily renewal, those patterns can be entirely shifted. God invites you, in partnership with science, to use scripture as a "thought prescription:" *"Do not be conformed to this world, but be transformed by the renewing of your mind…"* (Romans 12:2)

Speak softly: "Fear, you have no place here. God's love fills every empty space. I am safe, I am chosen, I am in covenant with life."

Invite the Holy Spirit to flood your heart with comfort and belief. Practice slow, deep breathing—a scientific method shown to lower stress and increase oxygen flow, which supports every system in the body (Thompson, 2015).

If you're struggling with doubt, chapter 11 provides a powerful activation that invites you to partner with Holy Spirit to unpack lies and unbelief. Ask God, "What lies am I believing? Where have I accepted less than Your promise?", What do I need to believe to hope in this area of my life"? Let the Holy Spirit gently teach, comfort, and break through old patterns. Repent of any agreement made with hopelessness, shame, or comparison. There is no condemnation in Christ. God loves you unconditionally, you could never let Him down.

Speak truth each day, no matter how you feel:

- "God's promise for me is abundant life."

- "I am not disqualified. I am chosen and beloved."

- "God's blessings are for me and my children."

Romans 8:11 beautifully affirms: *"And if the Spirit of Him who raised Jesus from the dead is living in you, He who raised Christ… will also give life to your mortal bodies…"* God's resurrection power is working in you, restoring, healing, and preparing every part of you for new life.

LIVING THE PROMISE: PRACTICING PROPHETIC SPEECH DAILY

The life-giving principle of prophecy—speaking God's truth in faith—can be transformative not merely as an occasional spiritual act, but as a daily practice. When longing for a baby, the discipline of speaking life is like watering a garden, nurturing seeds each day until fruit appears. Imagine your declarations as gentle rain: every time you speak a promise, it lands on the soil of your heart, nudging it toward new growth.

It may start quietly. Perhaps your first step is a simple affirmation whispered while making breakfast, or a scripture spoken softly at bedtime. Over time, this practice becomes a rhythm that undergirds your thinking, emotions, and bodily health. Neuroscience confirms: the repetition of positive, faith-rooted language rewires the brain, producing new connections that favour peace, resilience, and a readiness for miracles (Leaf, 2021; Amen, 2019).

As you meditate on God's word begin prophesying from it, for example, if your reading from Deuteronomy 28:2-4 which says, *"these blessings will come on you and accompany you if you obey the Lord your God: You will be blessed in the city and blessed in the country. The fruit of your womb will be blessed, and the crops of your land and the young of your livestock—the calves of your herds and the lambs of your flocks."*

You could prophesy over yourself and say, "I am blessed, I am blessed everywhere I go and my womb is blessed".

Journalling is another gentle but powerful way to integrate prophecy into your daily life. Write declarations and prayers, and then revisit them week by week. Document the moments when you sense hope sparking in your spirit—even minute ones. No breakthrough is too small to celebrate.

ACTIVATIONS: SPEAKING LIFE EACH DAY

Morning Practice

- Stand in front of a mirror, place your hand over your heart or womb, and declare:
  "God is giving life to me today—mind, body, and spirit. I receive His blessing."

- Speak a specific promise from scripture over your circumstances.

Midday Pause

- Pause midday and reflect: "Where do I need to invite life today? Where am I feeling stuck or dry?" Whisper a short prayer, inviting God's Spirit into that area.

Evening Reflections

- Write or share a testimony of a moment when you saw hope, life, or blessing in action. Thank God for every evidence of progress.

Weekly Community

- Join with a prayer group or trusted friend to share declarations. Pray for each other, listen for encouragement, and speak life into every heart.

Faith Declarations

- "God is always speaking life and hope into my story."

- "I am a fruitful vine, carrying blessing for generations (Psalm 128:3)."

- "Where there was despair, hope now springs forth."

- "No weapon formed against my body or destiny will prosper (Isaiah 54:17)."

- "My prayers are powerful, my words sow seeds of life, and God is with me."

QUESTIONS FOR REFLECTION

- Where am I believing more in my circumstances than in God's promise?

- What areas of my life feel "dry bones" today—how can I speak life into them?

- How am I partnering with God to call forth blessing and joy in my family?

- What do I need to believe to bring hope into this part of my life?

SCRIPTURES FOR MEDITATION

- Romans 4:17

- Ezekiel 37:1-14

- Exodus 23:26

- Psalm 113:9

- Psalm 128

- Genesis 17:7

- Romans 8:11

- Mark 11:23

SCRIPTURAL FOUNDATIONS: WHAT GOD SAYS ABOUT YOUR AUTHORITY TO GIVE LIFE

God's Word consistently affirms that life and renewal are within His will—and yours, through partnership. Consider these passages in fresh detail:

- **Deuteronomy 30:19:** "I have set before you life and death, blessings and curses. Now choose life, so that you and your children may live."
  Here, God sets out your authority. Choosing life is an active decision—made daily, moment by moment, especially in seasons of waiting.

- **Proverbs 15:4:** "The soothing tongue is a tree of life, but a perverse tongue crushes the spirit."
  Speaking kindly, gently to yourself and others brings healing, growth, and strength. Let gentleness shape your journey.

- **Jeremiah 1:10:** "See, today I appoint you…to build and to plant."

Your words have the ability to build and plant for the future. Every dec-laration sows, builds, and anticipates God's harvest in your family and your body.

DECLARATIONS AND MEDITATIONS

Before sleep, rest your head on a pillow of promises. Speak one or more of these gentle affirmations:

- "God's breath is in me—life flows where it once seemed dry."

- "I am worthy of blessing, healing, and fullness."

- "Even in silence, God is working—He brings forth new life in His time."

- "I rejoice in every small step, every sign, every seed of hope."

Let your meditations settle on these scriptures:

- **Psalm 103:5:** "Who satisfies your desires with good things so that your youth is renewed like the eagle's."

- **John 10:10:** "I have come that they may have life, and have it to the full."

- **Numbers 6:24-26:** "The Lord bless you and keep you; the Lord make his face shine on you and be gracious to you…"

LIFE FOR EVERY DAUGHTER

The power to call life into being rests not in your perfection, but in your relationship with God. He loves you unconditionally. Stand boldly in faith, speak blessing over yourself, and trust that your words—filled with Spirit and life—are planting seeds for your miracle. God's delight is to watch His daughters rise, hope, and bear fruit for generations.

No voice of doubt, fear, or shame can silence the gentle, powerful Holy Spirit who gives life to the hearts that wait, hope, and trust.

Let each moment and every word bring you deeper into your season of preparation, surrounded by God and His steadfast miracle-working love that gives life—to body, soul, and generations yet to come.

"Remember, this is a preparation season—you get to partner and create with God. There's no condemnation or guilt in your journey, only faith, hope, and love. Soak in God's presence, choose one or two Scriptures that speak to you, meditate on them, and listen to your favourite podcast or sermon.

I personally love listening to my spiritual parents, Steve and Wendy Backlund from Igniting Hope—their messages of hope are transformational, enlightening, and powerful. The goal isn't to feel overwhelmed, but to experience peace as you walk with God through this preparation season toward the conception and birth of your beautiful baby."

Chapter 10

Overshadow

"The Holy Spirit will come upon you, and the power of
the Most High will overshadow you"
— Luke 1:35

"God birthed the promise of Jesus in Mary, and I love Mary's humble response: *'Let it be to me according to Your word."* Mary's response is a word for you right now, God's will for your life is for you to have a baby, begin to declare, *"Lord let it be to me according to your word".*

Such a simple yet profound surrender holds the secret to walking through your preparation season with peace and power. Mary's words invite us to agree with God—to affirm that what He has birthed within us, even if unseen now, will come to pass.

The term "overshadow" in the scripture symbolises God's divine protection and manifestation of His glory, similar to a large umbrella shielding from the sun, but in this context, it highlights God's intervention in the miraculous conception of Jesus.

I prophesy over you that during your preparation season God's spirit overshadows you, your family, your mind, spirit and your womb keeping you shielded and protected under the shadows of His wings as you walk out this season with the Lord.

KEEP YOUR EYES ON THE WHO, NOT THE HOW

God's promise to Mary came with an incredible reassurance, echoed through Scripture for us all: *"Do not worry about tomorrow, but seek first the Kingdom of God and His righteousness, and all these things will be given to you"* (Matthew 6:34, 33).

What a powerful invitation—to release control over the "how" and keep our gaze steady on the "who": Jesus, the author and finisher of our faith (Hebrews 12:2), the One who bore our sins and established the new covenant through His blood. This promise can anchor your soul as you walk through the unknowns and uncertainties of waiting for your child.

Our preparation season often floods with questions—"How will this happen? When? God invites you gently to rest from wondering into resting in Him. Deep faith in the Lord requires us to surrender and trust that His timing, power, and plans are perfect.

RENEWING YOUR MIND—ELEVATING YOUR BELIEFS

God has already given us so much. The miracle begins when we lift our thoughts and beliefs higher—to align with His promises and authoritative word. *"Do not conform to the pattern of this world, but be transformed by the renewing of your mind,"* Paul commands (Romans 12:2).

This renewal ignites change in every sphere of your life—the spiritual, emotional, and physical. As I shared in previous chapters, Dr. Caroline Leaf, explains that our minds are neuroplastic, meaning they can be rewired through intentional thought and faith-filled declarations (Leaf, 2013). She affirms that attaching to God's truth and words helps to deactivate toxic thought patterns and build new, healthy neural pathways conducive to healing and breakthrough.

When you begin to raise your beliefs and thoughts to God's higher truth—that you are fearfully and wonderfully made (Psalm 139:14), that nothing is impossible with Him (Luke 1:37)—you invite God's power to move in your life. True surrender is both beautiful and liberating. It means laying down our striving and worries, and giving God's Spirit room to move freely and work in our lives.

In the same way God overshadowed Mary (Luke 1:35), His Holy Spirit desires to overshadow you—casting a protective, empowering shadow over your preparation season. To overshadow means to cover, protect, and enable by God's presence.

Imagine God's Spirit like a gentle umbrella shielding you from discouragement and fear, while flooding you with supernatural strength, grace, and courage that go beyond natural ability. This mysterious divine overshadowing sets you apart—for blessing, for promise, and for miracle.

MY TESTIMONY: WALKING UNDER HIS SHADOW

When I reflect on my preparation season, I learned to lean into His overshadowing power. My eyes were on the One who created me, knowing without a shadow of doubt that He would heal me, deliver me, and set me free. I didn't waver at His promises; I knew deep in my heart that if God did it for Sarah, Hannah, and even Elizabeth, He could do it for me.

The same Spirit that raised Jesus from the dead is the same Spirit who overshadowed me during my preparation season, and He overshadows you too. I know that if God did it for me, He can do it for you.

I began to notice new peace settling. I could rest more deeply. My words became softer, my faith stronger and excitement building within me because, just like Abraham in Romans 4:21, I was fully convinced of the promises of God. I realised I was no longer waiting alone—I was under a divine shadow of power and love.

SCIENTIFIC INSIGHTS: THE SHADOW OF THE HOLY SPIRIT AND THE BRAIN

Modern neuroscience sheds light on what the Bible calls "overshadowing." Dr. Curt Thompson describes the relational brain's capacity to be "activated" and "regulated" by connection with God and others (Thompson, 2015). The presence of the Holy Spirit—or even a close supportive community—engages neurobiological systems that reduce fear, increase oxytocin (the bonding hormone), and promote healing.

Dr. Leaf's research confirms that renewing thoughts with God's truth shifts brain chemistry, reducing stress responses (cortisol production) and encouraging neurogenesis (the creation of new brain cells), states conducive to physical health and emotional stability (Leaf, 2021).

This neurological "overshadowing" by Spirit translates into a real, measurable enabling power enabling hope, peace, and strength during long seasons of waiting.

SPEAKING LIFE AND POWER OVER YOUR PREPARATION

Your words, empowered by the Holy Spirit's overshadowing, are mighty. Speaking God's promises aloud aligns your spirit with heaven's rhythm. This is prophetic speech—it calls forth life out of seeming death.

Ask yourself daily: are the words coming from bitterness, fear, or frustration? Or are they reflections of God's truth and life? When doubt whispers, declare boldly:

- "I am overshadowed by God's Spirit—strengthened, protected, and empowered."
- "Life and blessing flow through my words and my womb."
- "I walk courageously in faith, hope, and love."

Consistently declaring such truths rewires your brain and opens your spirit to receive God's promises fully.

ACTIVATIONS: WELCOMING HIS OVERSHADOWING PRESENCE

Morning Whisper:
Place your hand on your womb or heart and quietly say,
"Holy Spirit, overshadow me with Your love and power. Fill me with strength for today."

Midday Breath:

When anxiety or weariness creeps in, take a deep breath. Visualise a warm shadow covering you, releasing peace and courage. Silent prayer:

"Cover me, Lord, with Your Holy Spirit's protection and grace."

Evening Reflection Journal:

Write three ways you sensed God's overshadowing during the day. Express gratitude for His presence.

Weekly Prayer Intercession:

Invite a prayer partner to declare scriptures about God's presence and overpowering strength over your preparation season.

DECLARATIONS TO SPEAK LOUDER THAN FEAR

- "God surrounds me with His shadow of peace and empowerment."

- "Every breath I take is filled with Spirit and life."

- "I receive strength beyond natural ability to carry this promise."

- "My womb and heart are covered by God's divine presence."

- "I walk forward boldly, confident in His covenant promises."

SCRIPTURES TO MEDITATE ON

- **Luke 1:35:** "The Holy Spirit will come upon you, and the power of the Most High will overshadow you."

- **Joshua 1:9:** "Be strong and courageous. Do not be afraid... for the Lord your God is with you wherever you go."

- **Psalm 91:4:** "He will cover you with His feathers, and under His wings you will find refuge."

- **Isaiah 40:31:** "But those who hope in the Lord will renew their strength."

- **2 Corinthians 12:9:** "My grace is sufficient for you, for my power is made perfect in weakness."

GENTLE ENCOURAGEMENT

Beloved daughter of God, your preparation season is sacred and filled with divine life. As Mary said, *"Let it be to me according to Your word"* (Luke 1:38), so also, may your heart surrender fully. Your words and faith create the soil for miracles to bloom. Let the Spirit overshadow you—protect, strengthen, and renew your mind and body as you wait expectantly.

Every breath you take, every word you speak is infused with spirit and life—the same Spirit that breathed life into dry bones and raised the dead. Your journey is being transformed moment by moment.

You are held, treasured, and empowered by the God who calls things into existence that don't yet appear. Walk gently, speak boldly, and receive peace.

Chapter 11

Renewing the Mind

Be transformed by the renewing of your mind.
— Romans 12:2

We speak, on average, around 16,000 words a day, and researchers estimate we have roughly 6,000–6,200 distinct thoughts each day. That is an incredible amount of thinking and speaking for one person.

How many of those thoughts are you consciously aware of? Romans 12:2 says, *"Be transformed by the renewing of your mind."* What thoughts are you renewing your mind with? Are they thoughts that uplift you and bring you peace and joy, or are they thoughts of worry or fear.

In this chapter, I want to share an activation I've used countless times—whenever God reveals a lie I've believed and gently leads me to renew my mind with His truth. This simple tool helps you unpack any lies that surface, surrender them to God, and replace them with life-giving declarations of His Word.

It's an essential practice for your preparation season toward the conception and birth of your precious baby. But this is more than a one-time tool—it's a lifestyle. You can use it in every area of your life, for the rest of your life, to partner with God in renewing your mind and walking in freedom (Romans 12:2).

THOUGHT, FEELING, ACTION

All throughout the Word, God speaks about how powerful our words are. They start as thoughts and then we begin to speak them. A thought becomes a feeling, and a feeling becomes an action. For example, we can have a thought of joy; that thought of joy becomes a feeling, and that feeling becomes an action that shows up in our life and we express it through being happy.

On the other hand, we can think a thought of worry; that worry becomes a feeling, which is often fear and that feeling becomes an action that can reflect in our circumstances and can stop us from moving forward in life.

When we renew our mind with positive or negative thoughts, they often reflect in our circumstances. Sometimes we can renew our mind with a fear or a lie, and then it becomes a belief that shows up our circumstances. Discouragement and fear can take a grip when we renew our minds with lies. Those lies, over time, become strongholds, and that is exactly what they do—they hold strongly onto your mind and become beliefs that reflect in your circumstances.

We can have thoughts and beliefs that are strongholds that are both positive and negative, just as we we can renew our minds with God's truth and promises we can renew our minds with lies. When we become a new creation in Christ, we are invited by God to renew our minds from old patterns of thinking to new patterns of thinkings that align with His word and His promises for us.

Renewing our minds with new beliefs about who we are requires us to surrender old beliefs, we can't begin to renew our minds with God's truth if we don't believe who God says we are and all that we acquire as new creations in Christ. For example, if we are renewing our minds with the truth that we are worthy but don't believe it than we will be unable to receive it and be transformed.

Transformation comes from believing something different. We first must repent of believing the lie that we are unworthy, surrender this to Jesus and begin declaring who God says we are by renewing our minds with the truth "I am worthy".

THE SCIENCE OF THE BRAIN AND STRONGHOLDS

Science tells us that the brain is changeable; this is called neuroplasticity. God-designed our brain's with the ability to form new neural pathways and change its structure based on repeated thoughts and experiences. Every time you think a thought, especially one you repeat often, your brain strengthens that pathway, making that thought easier to think again. Over time, repeated thoughts become mental "default settings."

A stronghold, in both biblical and practical terms, is a fortified pattern of thinking—a system of beliefs lodged in the mind that exerts a powerful grip over us and defends its right to there. My spiritual father, Steve Backlund, teaches that strongholds are established belief systems formed through repeated thoughts and words (Romans 10:17), and they can be both positive and negative.

Negative strongholds consist of lies and limiting beliefs that block transformation and create areas lacking hope and one begins to feel hope deferred (Proverbs 13:12).

Positive strongholds, however, are empowering truths we build by aligning with God's Word that brings hope just as Romans 15:13 says, *"May the God of hope fill. You with all joy and peace as you trust in him"*. Like a mental fortress constructed through repeated agreement over time, these strongholds profoundly shape our emotions, actions, and sense of unchangeable reality & truth.

2 Corinthians 10:4–5 speaks of this battle: *"The weapons of our warfare are not carnal but mighty in God for pulling down strongholds, casting down arguments and every high thing that exalts itself against the knowledge of God, and taking every thought captive to the obedience of Christ."*

This means that, with the Holy Spirit and God's Word—as Steve Backlund emphasises, through using declarations to "tear down negative strongholds and set up positive strongholds"—you can literally partner with how your brain works. You replace old thought patterns with new, truth-filled ones, forming neural pathways that align with the mind of Christ (Romans 12:2).

IDENTITY & BELIEFS

I believed many lies about myself. I believed I was too old to be a mum. I believed the lie that I would never be a good mum, which made me believe another lie—that I could never be a mother at all. I renewed my mind with these lies for many years, and they became my "truth," which then reflected in my circumstances.

The thought that I was too old to be a mum became a feeling, and that feeling became my action and confession. I began saying, "I will never be a mum," and, "I am a career woman, I don't have time for children." However, deep down, I desired children more than anything but because of the fears I had and the lies I believed about myself and my circumstances, I didn't believe it was possible for me—this was never God's promise for my life.

This principle can be used in every area of your life. Steve Backlund, speaks about renewing the mind. He shares that deep, lasting transformation in our lives comes from surrendering our beliefs. Frances Frangipane shares this: *"Every area of our lives that doesn't glisten with hope means you are believing a lie, and that area is a stronghold of the devil in your life."*

I began a journey of asking the Lord to reveal every lie I was believing about me, my life, my circumstances and He gently began to unravel them one by one. The thoughts that had been running through my mind—thoughts I had partnered with for many years—started to come to the surface. These were lies that stood in direct opposition to His Word about me and to His promises as my Father and to me as His daughter.

For many years, I couldn't understand why I wasn't seeing transformation in my life. After all, I am a new creation in Christ; I no longer live, but Christ lives in me. Then why wasn't this truth reflecting in my life? I received the revelation that I won't see transformation if I don't believe it. I asked the Lord what lies I was believing about myself. He revealed many lies, one being that I didn't believe I was good enough. He then began to reveal where I first believed that lie—which was when I was a child. I repented of believing the lie and then began to renew my mind with His truth. Once He revealed the lies, I began to unpack them with Holy Spirit, surrender them to the cross, and speak daily declarations that renewed my mind with God's truth about who I am.

Next, I want to show you this powerful activation—a lifestyle, not a one-time event—that you can use in every area of your life, including renewing your mind with the belief of carrying your beautiful baby and embracing what God says about who you are.

Some powerful scriptures to stand on as you renew your mind include:

- Romans 12:2 – "Do not be conformed to this world, but be transformed by the renewing of your mind."

- 2 Corinthians 10:4–5 – "The weapons of our warfare are… mighty in God for pulling down strongholds… taking every thought captive to the obedience of Christ."

- Philippians 4:8 – "Whatever is true, whatever is noble… think about such things."

- Ephesians 4:23 – "Be renewed in the spirit of your mind."

ACTIVATION

During the following activation, have your journal with you so you can write down what the Holy Spirit shows you in your imagination or what you hear. Ask the following questions and record what

He reveals. For the first time you do this activation, set aside an hour in your quiet time with the Lord to go through it slowly.

To begin to relax, put on some gentle Christian instrumental soaking music and invite the Holy Spirit to fill the space with His peace. Take slow, deep breaths, inviting your whole being to rest in God's presence. As you breathe, speak kindly to your body and tell it to relax, noticing any areas of tension, then breathing into those places and letting them soften. You can also hold a book loosely in your hands whilst keeping your grip relaxed. Begin by asking the Holy Spirit the following;

1. ***Holy Spirit what is an area of my life where you want to increase my hope.***

(Journal what you hear or see)

2. ***Holy Spirit what is the lie I am believing about this area of my life?***

In this process of the activation, you may get an image or hear a word from the Lord, trust that you are hearing from the Lord and try not to overthink it, again, write down what you hear or see, allow Holy Spirit to reveal what it is, He is so gentle and loving, He will only show you what you are ready for.

I often go deeper with Holy Spirit and ask Him, "When did the lie get in?", "Did something happen in my childhood"?, "Was there something I was taught"? These are good question to ask because we want to get to the root of the lie and allow the Lord to pull it out for good.

If you are struggling to believe that you are called to be a mother than you could ask Holy Spirit the following questions;

Holy Spirit, am I believing any lies about being a mother? Holy Spirit, reveal every lie I believe about myself.

Give yourself grace—this process takes time. The Lord may reveal a lie in that moment and, as you continue asking this question, He will gently uncover further lies you have believed about yourself and your circumstances. Focus on working through one lie at a time and renewing your mind with God's truth and promises. The following activation in this chapter will show you how.

FORGIVENESS

During this process, if you sense a blockage, it can sometimes indicate there may be someone you need to forgive. Forgiveness is not easy, especially when we have been deeply hurt, but it is a powerful part of healing. Forgiveness means taking your power back; when you forgive, you are choosing to release that person and the hold they have had over your heart. At times, you may need to forgive yourself or even God (not because He has done wrong, but because your heart has held offence).

Scripture calls us to forgive others as we have been forgiven: *"Be kind and compassionate to one another, forgiving each other, just as in Christ God forgave you"* (Ephesians 4:32). Forgiveness does not mean you have to allow someone back into your life or trust them again; it simply means you are breaking connection and releasing them into God's hands. For some, this is a process that takes time and repeated surrender. At the end of this book, I have included a forgiveness prayer you can use if the Holy Spirit reveals someone you need to forgive.

When God leads me to forgive someone, I pray a forgiveness prayer and visualise a spiritual cord—like an umbilical cord—being severed in the spiritual realm. Then I bless and pray for the person, as Scripture says *"Bless those who curse you, pray for those who mistreat you"* (Luke 6:28). Its never an easy process but it is so freeing and I know that Jesus is always comforting me during this process of my healing.

RENOUNCE & REPENT

The next step in this process is to renounce & repent for the lie. Renouncing the lie simply means intentionally breaking your agreement with it—confessing that it is not from God, rejecting its power over you, and choosing to agree with God's truth about who you are instead. Repenting means turning away from it with a complete change of mind and heart, no longer agreeing with it and choosing God's truth instead.

In the name of Jesus, I nail to the cross the lie

____ .

And I break all agreements known and unknown I made with the lie ____ .

I repent for joining with this lie and I command all darkness and deception away from me.

I thank you Father for removing all this away from me as far as the east is from the west.

Close your eyes and surrender the lie to Jesus. This is where He will show you what He does with it. In this process I close my eyes and visualise giving Jesus the lie, I often see Him holding the lie on a piece of paper with the roots attached to it and then he burns it, I believe He shows me this to indicate that He has pulled the lie out by the roots and then He burns it to show that He has dealt with the lie for good.

This next part of the activation is the exciting part, this is where we get to invite Holy Spirit in to speak the truth over you.

GOD'S TRUTH & DECLARATIONS

Next, close your eyes and ask the Lord the following:

- "Lord, show me the truth: _______________________________."
  Or

- "Holy Spirit give me a picture of the truth?"
  _______________________________.

- "Jesus, what do you want to replace this lie with"?
  _______________________________.

- "God, Who do You say I am?"
  _______________________________.

You can choose one of the questions above or all of them. I like to ask Holy Spirit all of the questions above and wait on Him to reveal the truth of who I am. I grew up in a dysfunctional home & community, so Holy Spirit often shows me an image from my childhood where the lie got in and replaces it with His beautiful truth.

Hold your hands out and ask Jesus to give you a vision of the truth. It is so powerful when you close your eyes and ask the Lord to show you a vision of the truth. As I shared in previous chapters, my spiritual mother, Wendy Backlund says that faith is the womb of your imagination; I love this because the brain "sees" the image more deeply and creates a new neural pathway that you get to renew your mind, with God's word and promises, partnering with how God designed your brain to change and heal.

Faith is now, in this present moment that God is doing what He says He is doing; Scripture says in Hebrews 11:1, "*Now faith is the confidence in what we hope for and assurance about what we do not see.*" Faith says we believe first, then we will see the fruits.

Holy Spirit will never re-traumatise or trigger you; He has such a beautiful and gentle approach to revealing the lie and then replacing it with the truth. I encourage you to take your time with this process and allow Jesus to bring healing.

I have often felt Jesus healing my heart during this activation and seen Him in my imagination holding my heart in His hands—as "*the eyes of my imagination are enlightened to see the glorious inheritance and power I am called into*" (Ephesians 1:18). It is such a beautiful process where you will never be the same; receive the healing from Jesus by faith.

Then ask the Lord, "*Lord, what are some declarations I can say to renew my mind with Your truth?*"

Some example declarations might include:

- "I am a beloved daughter of God." (1 John 3:1)

- "I am fruitful and blessed in my body and family." (Deuteronomy 28:4, Psalm 128:3)

- "I have the mind of Christ." (1 Corinthians 2:16)

- "I am a wonderful Mother"

Speak these out loud. Remember, you are already speaking around 16,000 words a day; imagine the impact when more and more of those words agree with God's truth and His word rather than the enemy's lies.

When you speak God's promises out loud—declaring life over your womb, your waiting, your miracle—and hear your own voice, your brain actually forges stronger pathways than when you merely think them silently in your head.

This is because you're activating more parts of your brain simultaneously: the regions that move your mouth to speak and the ones that hear and process sound, creating a powerful multi-sensory loop. It's like the difference between reading about riding a bike and actually peddling down the road—engaging more senses together builds deeper neural connections, helping you remember and believe those truths on a cellular level.

Couple this with Wendy Backlund's profound insight that "the imagination is the womb of faith," and it becomes supernatural: as you declare aloud, engage your spiritual eyes by vividly imagining what you're speaking—your baby kicking in the womb, your arms full, the cry of new life filling the room.

This added sense of Spirit-led visualisation doesn't just anchor the promise; it births faith right there in the unseen realm, making heaven's reality feel as tangible as your own heartbeat.

2 Corinthians 4:18 says, *"So we fix our eyes not on what is seen, but on what is unseen, since what is seen is temporary, but what is unseen is eternal."*

FINAL WORDS

Renewing the mind Is a powerful process. What you believe shapes how you see God, yourself, your future, and even your journey to motherhood. The beautiful truth is that, in Christ, your mind is not stuck. Your brain can change, your patterns can change, and your story can change and you have the power and authority to do so.

Through the Holy Spirit, the Word of God, and simple daily choices to reject lies and agree with truth, you are actively rewiring your brain and renewing your mind. Every time you take a thought captive, surrender a lie, and replace it with God's Word, you are pulling down a stronghold and building a fortress of truth in its place. Every declaration of God's promise over your life, your womb, and your future baby is another brick of hope laid in that fortress.

You and your beautiful baby story are not defined by past lies, delays, or disappointments. You are being transformed, from the inside out, by the renewing of your mind. Keep going. Keep agreeing with heaven. Your thoughts, your words, and your beliefs are aligning with God's heart—and that alignment is powerful.

Final Thoughts

A Season of Hope and Joy

Your preparation season toward the conception and birth of your beautiful baby is a sacred journey. It is marked by hope that does not disappoint, faith that stands firm, and love that sustains.

When the doctors shared the wonderful news with me that I was pregnant with Noah, tears streamed down my face. The doctor asked, *"Are you not happy?"* I laughed through my tears and said, *"No, I am very happy—these are tears of joy."*

God had come through. I partnered with Him and it was my faith, hope, love and trust in Him that opened the door to God birthing my beautiful son and the belief of His powerful word and promises.

I am so grateful for my son Noah, and I am deeply grateful for my journey and my preparation season—that led us to this miracle.

My prayer for you now as you delight in the Lord is this: "Delight yourself in the Lord, and he will give you the desires of your heart".

Psalms 37:4. May you walk forward boldly, filled with the joy and peace that only His Spirit can give. May your heart be confident, your mind renewed, and your womb blessed abundantly.

Your miracle is on its way.

Blessings and love,
Cheree xx

My Testimony

In revelations 19:10 it says, *"The testimony of Jesus is the the spirit of prophecy"*, this scripture releases a prophecy of my testimony to the reader. Sharing my testimony throughout my book releases to you a prophecy that speaks over you the blessings of a baby.

I grew up in broken home, but I always knew deep in my spirit that there was more to life than what I was seeing, living and experiencing. I was 39 when I had a supernatural encounter with God, at the time I was questioning whether God existed and I didn't believe in Jesus.

I was fighting suicidal ideations and the torment of the sexual abuse I had been through as a child plagued me and I was always searching for peace in all the wrong places. I was into new age practices for 20 years prior, not knowing that I was partnering with dark realms.

My dear friend, invited me to the healing rooms for prayer, the healing rooms are a place where different people from all denominations come together and provide a sanctuary of prayer where the spirit of God can bring healing, love and comfort.

I felt like a fish out of water when I attended the healing rooms, I was way out of my comfort zone. Two beautiful ladies prayed over me that day, a prayer that changed my life forever. They prayed a prayer inviting Jesus to break of trauma in every area of my life and my body, it was when they prayed, *"In the name of Jesus we break of trauma from the moment of conception"*, I burst into tears. When I stopped crying, peace washed over me and I felt a freedom I had never known before.

From that day forward Jesus moved in my life in such beautiful and incredible ways and I left my old life behind.

I find it profoundly powerful that the first healing and deliverance prayer I received—breaking trauma off me from the very moment of my conception—marked the divine beginning of my preparation season.

Years later, God has positioned my testimony to help awaken faith in other women for their own conception and motherhood. I stand as living testimony to God's unwavering faithfulness—He healed my life, restored my womb, and blessed me with my beautiful son Noah.

If God did it for me, He can do it for you, I want to repeat that scripture again so that you catch it in your spirit, *"The testimony of Jesus is the spirit of prophesy"*, Revelation 19:10. Wow, The testimony that I have of what Jesus did for me, prophesies into your life and when He does this for you in your preparation season, your testimony will prophesy into other peoples lives and set's them free.

Sister, I truly believe that if you're holding this book right now, this is the beautiful beginning of your preparation season where God's promises for your family are taking root. I'm overflowing with joy and excitement for you—I'm praying for you and I bless you. Get ready—open your heart wide, because our faithful God is about to move in your life in the most breathtaking, miraculous ways.

Blessings & Love,
Cheree xx

Journalling with Jesus

Forgiveness Prayer

Prayer of Forgiveness to Those Who Have Harmed Me

Lord, I choose to forgive ____(name)____________________ for

____

Lord, I give You permission to take the judgment and bitterness out of my life. I do not want this in my life. I surrender it to you and ask you to remove it, to heal me where I have been wounded, and to forgive me where I have sinned. I choose also to forgive myself.

I choose not to blame or hold the action of ____________________ against him/her. Where I have been betrayed, I ask You to remove the arrows, to heal me, and to restore trust.

I hereby surrender my right to be paid back for my loss by the one show has sinned against me, and in so doing I declare my trust in You alone God as the righteous Judge.

Father, please bless ______________________ In every way!

In Jesus' Heavenly name, Amen

Endnote

If you are reading this book, you have already taken a step of faith—you love the Lord and desire to walk in obedience to His commandments. The core of His commandments is simple yet profound: to love God with all your heart, soul, mind, and strength, and to love your neighbour as yourself (Mark 12:30-31). And if you haven't yet accepted Jesus as your Lord & Saviour, I encourage you with all my heart to give your life to Him today, your life will never be the same.

Sources & References

Scripture quotations taken from THE HOLY BIBLE, NEW INTERNATIONAL VERSION®, NIV®

Copyright © 1973, 1978, 1984, 2011 by Biblica, Inc.®

Used by permission. All rights reserved worldwide. *Romans 12:2; 4:17, 20-22; 15:13; 8:1-2, 11, 28, 37*

Holy Bible, New King James Version (NKJV).
Thomas Nelson, 1982.
Primary source for all Scripture quotations including:
2 Corinthians 10:4-5; 1:20; 5:7; 12:9

- Ephesians 4:23, 29; 1:18

- Luke 1:35-45; 1:13-17, 41-42

- Hebrews 11:1; 6:19; 13:5

- James 1:12; 2:22; 3:2-12; 5:16

- Proverbs 13:12; 18:21; 21:23; 4:23; 15:4

- Psalm 127:3; 128:3; 139:13-16, 14; 91:4; 34:4-5; 103:5; 1:2; 100:4

- Deuteronomy 7:9, 13; 28:2-4; 30:19; 31:6

- Genesis 1:3, 17, 18:12, 21:1-2

- Isaiah 55:11; 66:9; 40:31; 43:19; 54:17

- Mark 9:23; 11:23; 13:16

- Matthew 6:10, 33-34; 28:20

- John 6:63; 14:12; 10:10

- 1 Samuel 1:27; 1 John 3:1; 1 Corinthians 2:16, 13

- Joshua 1:8-9; Numbers 23:19; Jeremiah 29:11; Exodus 23:26

- Ezekiel 37:1-14

- 2 Corinthians 10:4-5; 1:20; 5:7; 12:9

Strong's Concordance. Referenced throughout for Hebrew (emunah H530, aman H539) and Greek (pistis G4102, pisteuō G4100, anakainōsis G342, episkiazō G1982) word studies. BibleHub.com.

SCIENTIFIC AND NEUROSCIENCE SOURCES

- **Big Think.** "New study suggests we have 6,200 thoughts every day." April 18, 2022. https://bigthink.com/neuropsych/how-many-thoughts-per-day/bigthink

- **Healthline.** "How Many Thoughts Do You Have Per Day? And Other FAQs." February 27, 2022. https://www.healthline.com/health/how-many-thoughts-per-dayhealthline

- **Leaf, Dr. Caroline.** *Switch On Your Brain*. Baker Books, 2013.
  Additional teachings on neuroplasticity, 21-day renewal

cycles, and thought restructuring (2018, 2021). https://drleaf.
comrodgerscc

- **American Psychological Association.** Articles on hope, positive psychology, and placebo effect (2018). https://www.apa.org

- **American Society for Reproductive Medicine.** "Stress and Infertility." 2022. https://www.asrm.org/topics/topics-index/stress/

- **Journal of Psychosomatic Obstetrics & Gynecology.** "Impact of stress, anxiety, and emotional well-being on fertility outcomes." 2020.

- **Thompson, Dr. Curt.** Referenced research on relational brain activation, oxytocin, breathing techniques, and stress reduction (2015).

- **Amen, Dr. Daniel.** Referenced studies on brain imaging, neural pathways, and faith/optimism (2019).

- **Rodgers Christian Counselling.** "Rewire Your Brain with Biblical Principles and Neuroscience." https://www.rodgerscc.com/re-wire-your-brain-with-biblical-principles-and-neuroscience/rodgerscc

- **Inspiring Lives Magazine.** "Renewing Your Mind: Where Faith Meets Neuroscience." October 12, 2024. https://www.inspiringlivesmagazine.com/health-wellness/renewing-your-mind-where-faith-meets-neuroscience/inspiringlivesmagazine

CHRISTIAN AUTHORS AND MINISTRY TEACHINGS

- **Backlund Leadership Academy.** (n.d.). *Beliefs Training* [Online course/Zoom session]. Igniting Hope Ministries. **https://backlundleadershipacademy.com/**

- **Backlund, Steve.** *Igniting Hope Ministries.* Teachings on renewing the mind, positive/negative strongholds, declarations, hope ("believing the future will be better"), and prophetic testimony. Various resources including "Writing Your Own Declarations" (2024). https://www.ignitinghope.com

- **Backlund, Wendy.** Referenced quotes: "Faith is the womb/seed of our imagination." Igniting Hope Ministries teachings.

- **Frangipane, Francis.** "Every area of our lives that doesn't glisten with hope means you are believing a lie." Teachings on hope and strongholds.

ADDITIONAL THEOLOGICAL RESOURCES

- **GotQuestions.org.** Articles on spiritual strongholds, faith (pistis), biblical hope, power of words, and supernatural promises. https://www.gotquestions.orggotquestions

- **Desiring God.** Teachings including "The Battle for Your Mind" and "The Renewed Mind and How to Have It" (2025). https://www.desiringgod.org

- **Awesome Church.** "Breaking Strongholds of the Mind." 2023. https://www.awesomechurch.com/breaking-strongholds-of-the-mind-part-1/awesomechurch

- **MacLeod & Forrin** (2017) meta-review: Active vocal production makes info "distinct in long-term memory," outperforming passive methods.

Cognitive Psychology studies (e.g., 2012): Verbalising aloud identifies errors 40% faster, generates 27% more solutions by organising thoughts externally.

Baddeley's phonological loop model: Speaking reduces cognitive load, freeing resources for reasoning.